GROW INTO
INVESTING
WISDOM

*A Psychosocial Guide to Building
Wealth through Personal Development*

DR. RICARDO FAINSILBER

Quick guide of the stages

Stage	Tasks	Investment Crisis	Central Process	Investor Adaptive Quality	Core Issue
Ingenuous Impetus	1. Maturation of understanding the basics of investing 2. Developing respect for the risks involved 3. Emotional development	Fearful versus imprudent	Replication	Hope	Dropping out as an investor
Unfolding acumen of inquiry	1. Developing the investor's self-concept 2. Skill learning 3. Maturation of decision-making biases 4. Sense of belonging to a peer group	Drive Vs. Inadequacy	Education	Proficiency	Idleness
Sophisticated skills, sound identity	1. Work discipline and management of life's demands 2. Lifestyle and investment 3. Investment philosophy	Spreading out vs. Aridness	Inventiveness	Commitment	Neglect
Weathered Investor	1. Embracing one's life 2. Adopting new roles and new investment perspectives 3. Getting future generations involved 4. Planning a legacy	Appeasement vs. Despondency	Contemplation	Insight	Condescension

ISBN: 978-1-7365101-0-0

Dedication

To the main players who have supported
my education and my investment endeavors
—Salomon, Jacqueline, Erika, and Claudia.

This book is dedicated to Jeremy and Emily. May you
grow healthy and wealthy to become insightful,
thoughtful, and responsible individuals.

"Wisdom is not a product of schooling but of the lifelong attempt to acquire it."

— Albert Einstein

"Socratic self-knowledge means working on oneself, with others, to become the sort of person who could know himself, and thus be responsible to the world, to others, and to oneself, intellectually, morally, and practically."

— Christopher Moore, from *Socrates and Self-knowledge*

CONTENTS

CHAPTER 1

Foundations

Before diving into the theory and the story postulated by this book, I'll share some general thoughts on investing, wealth building, and becoming an investor. This book is written for people who intend to become investors, which is usually motivated by the ambition of increasing wealth or income. This book indeed teaches what a person needs to develop proficiency as an investor. However, it's important to note that some things that seem unrelated to the abilities of wealth building have significant importance in an investor's journey.

The term *investor* will be used a great deal throughout the book, so it's important to clearly understand what it means to be an investor. A basic dictionary definition is: "A person who puts money into something in order to make a profit or get an advantage."[1] However, this book's perspective on what it means to be an investor is broader than this stated definition. The definition of investor for this book incorporates three important aspects: commitment of resources, how work is involved, and types of investment.

Regarding the first of these three aspects, an *investor* is a person who commits personal resources to a plan drafted with the intention of gaining something. Money is certainly an important resource and measure of value and will almost always be involved

---

[1] "Investor," *Cambridge Advanced Learner's Dictionary & Thesaurus.*

in an investment. But people have other resources that must be included in their plans to make an investment successful. An investor compromises time, energy, knowledge, and experience to make a decision. All of those resources need to be invested alongside money.

Second, sometimes people invest only time and/or energy with the intent to make a profit, which is typically called *work*. Working at a company or institution is a type of investment that doesn't necessarily involve putting money in, but resources are definitely invested. In physics, though, work is done whenever a force causes a displacement.[2] When it comes to people utilizing force, they have invested their resources into applying that force. What all this means is that investing and work cannot be separated. Investments that do not include appropriate amounts of work will fail.

Finally, an investor is typically thought of as someone who knows finance and invests money in the public markets full time. However, that is a reductionistic view of what it means to be an investor because there are many ways to invest. People can invest privately in businesses and other assets. And investing doesn't have to be in large sums, nor does it have to be their main activity. The possibilities in the stock market are massive, but the options to invest privately are even wider.

Someone who buys a car and rents it out to an Uber driver is as much of an investor as someone who buys a vacation house and earns by making it an Airbnb. Also, someone who has a full-time job but buys a self-storage facility every other year is an investor, just like someone who decides to become a full-time crypto currencies speculator. Imagination and creativity are the only limits to the investment possibilities a person can find.

To become a good investor, a person must strive to grow internally. Personal development should go hand in hand with

---

[2] Glenn Elert, "What Is Work?," *The Physics Hypertextbook.*

wealth growth, so the wealth can be sustainable in the long term. Personal growth around investments is related to the emotional maturity, knowledge, and experience of investing. Internal/personal development is much more difficult to measure than material assets. Yet in the context of investing, this type of growth can be achieved through the tasks presented in the stages of this book's theory. When the wealth growth is asymmetric or out of balance with personal growth, the only thing that will increase is frustration because the wealth will diminish.

As mentioned above, the book is organized into chapters that describe different stages in an investor's development. Such descriptions are based on concepts derived from psychosocial theory. The main concepts that will be used in the theory chapters include the following:

1. **Tasks**. A (*developmental) task* is a goal that arises during a certain period of the lifespan.
2. **Investment Crisis**. An *investment crisis* occurs when someone's coping mechanisms are not enough to resolve a stressful situation that is common to a given stage of development.
3. **Central Process**. The *central process* is a series of things that will naturally occur to help the investor resolve the crisis they're facing.
4. **Investor Adaptive Quality**. An *investor adaptive quality* is a new, adaptive coping strategy that arises if an investment crisis is resolved positively.
5. **Core Issue**. A *core issue* is a problem that will emerge if a crisis is resolved ineffectively.

This book will certainly help you learn about how to develop as an investor. Yet one thing that I'd like readers to note before jumping into the investment world is that money will not solve your problems. Everybody needs money to live, and having more money can certainly open up more options and provide some comfort. Yet without the proper internal/personal development, money will only accentuate inner voids. It's also worth noting that having more money means having more responsibility. And if you don't embrace responsibility accordingly, you will lose the money faster than what it took to make it.

Building wealth is neither quick nor easy. It involves work (effort), and getting started requires you to keep a job or business as you begin your investment journey. Later on, becoming a full-time investor could become an option. However, if you want to become an investor, I recommend you search for investments that are not connected to your job or business. Investing in your own business is not really investing—it is growing your business. That makes sense for an entrepreneur, but that is not investing because it only increases their workload. To have a sound investment strategy, an investor should look for uncorrelated investments to strengthen their financial positioning.

An investor needs to learn how to put their resources to work for themselves. Work is always necessary, but how much an investor wants to work should be up to them rather than how much time others require of them. That brings up the point of differentiating between being an investor and being an entrepreneur: entrepreneurs take on the operations of a single business, while investors can invest in many businesses and do not get involved in operations.

There is a common stereotype that investors are very wealthy people who do not work. Many think that the only thing they need to do is make a call here and there or push a few buttons on their computers and voilà! More money in their accounts. But just like most other stereotypes, this could not be further from reality. Sure, investors may not be involved in a business's operation, but investing can still involve a lot of work.

First of all, one does not need to be wealthy to be an investor. It's possible to become an investor with just $100 USD. Also, to become a successful investor, a lot of time and effort are needed to complete the necessary tasks and achieve maturity as an investor.

Additional effort aside, being an investor does allow for heightened control of the investor's resources, including their time.

Finally, this last idea is not easy to assimilate for an aspiring or beginner investor, as it seems counterintuitive. But to a more seasoned investor, investing is never about the money. As a person becomes a more mature investor, money becomes a simple, symbolic scale that allows investors to measure what they have achieved. The numbers represent results, tell stories, and provide a system for understanding what went on with an investment. A mature investor who truly has a passion for investments is never thinking about pulling money out of their investments. They really can never have enough money, time, or energy to keep looking for and making new investments. But those new investments will, in time, become stories that will be told through the symbolic value of numbers.

The Developmental Perspective

Just as each individual and their life story are unique, each investor and their investment journey are one of a kind. Studying investors' ventures can help elucidate common characteristics seen in many individuals who have gone through a similar path. And while in no way is the individual aspect less important than the commonalities, learning about analogous traits in different investors can help us identify collective patterns of transition and trans-formation that investors must navigate.

This book follows a developmental approach based on the psychosocial theory. A developmental approach refers to the process an individual has to navigate to grow and evolve as a person. Just like any living being experiences changes and transformations as they develop, an investor will need to engage in a developmental process to grow into a more mature investor. Investors will go through a series of crises that stem from the conflict of their old selves and their new abilities and attitudes that are constantly shifting and expanding. Each crisis that happens represents a stage that the investor is navigating; navigating these stages is also called life cycles.

The goal of the developmental approach of the book is to understand how investors make sense of their experiences, adapt to situations, cope with challenges, and continue to develop from one stage to the next. Understanding the developmental path will give an edge to an aspiring investor. Each person's investment journey is unique because it is shaped by a person's gender, ethnicity, culture, health, education, socioeconomic background, family history, sexual orientation, physical abilities and disabilities, geographical location, and, of course, historical, political, and economic contexts.

The systematic study of lifespan development dates back to the late 1800s. Prominent contributors to the field perhaps start with Charles Darwin and extend through writings of Wilhelm Preyer, Jean Piaget, Lev Vygotsky, and John Bowlby. The work of these last three authors—Piaget, Vygotsky, and Bowlby—specifically created the field of developmental psychology. Important contributions to the understanding of life development, and perhaps more widely known at present, were also conceived by Sigmund Freud, Erik Erikson, and Carl Jung. The field of developmental psychology has grown and evolved over a century, and it has influenced countless aspects of our lives.

Through the work of these formidable and influential scholars, as well as other developmentalists, certain related principles can be defined and should be used in any study with a developmental perspective, which is the case for this book.

1. **Growth lasts throughout our whole lifespan.** Every stage of growth is influenced by what happened before and will have an effect on what occurs next. At every stage, new challenges will surface and have to be dealt with, resulting in the emergence of a new perspective. An important concept to consider in a lifespan development study is

plasticity, which means there is a capacity for reorganization, which can occur at neurological, psychological, and behavioral levels.

2. **Growth is multi-dimensional and multi-directional.** Different dimensions that experience growth are biological, psychological, and social. Growth is also multi-directional because sometimes when one area grows, another might lag behind. For example, a stock investor who decides to focus on learning and getting involved with real estate investing might experience growth in that direction but could be falling behind with stock market investing.

3. **The relative influence of biology and experience changes as the life cycle progresses.** While biological functions such as energy level, mind sharpness, and general body function tend to weaken over time, the level of experience, education, and knowledge tend to increase and, up to certain point, compensate.

4. **Developing or growing implies a redistribution of resources.** People invest their personal resources such as time, energy, money, talent, and social connections in different ways. Said resources can be used for growth, maintenance, recovery, or in facing a loss when maintaining or recovering are not possible. The resource allocation for these functions changes throughout the lifespan, especially when the resources become scarce. In early stages, most resources are used for growth, while in middle stages they are used for maintenance. Then in advanced stages, resources are used to regulate losses. In the context of investors, I don't mean older, more experienced investors will be dealing more often with losing capital. Yet they will have to invest personal resources in dealing with losses such as drive, ambition, motivation, or work capacity. Those fourteen-hour workdays they once endured are no longer feasible.

5. **Historical and cultural context influence development.**
    Every individual grows in many contexts or circumstances
    defined in part by maturity and in part by place and time.
    People have an influence in their environment as much as
    they are influenced by it. The meaning of any behavior
    change must be interpreted in light of the environment
    where it occurs.

I have chosen to highlight these five key principles because
they help us understand the developmental stages (especially what
is central in each stage) and the related tasks outlined in the coming
chapters. As you read through the book, you'll notice there is a
common structure in the theory chapters. The book structure will
become familiar and, while it is important to read through the
whole book, after a first read, each element in the stages'
descriptions will become an individual reference item for you to
revisit when needed.

CHAPTER 2

A Developmental Perspective

This chapter offers context about what it means to have a developmental perspective on life and in investing. All components of this multifaceted psychosocial theory are clearly described. And there's discussion about concepts basic to the theory and to the structure of the stages' descriptions. These insights are vital to understand before learning how they all play out in each stage of development.

Psychosocial Approach: Interaction of Biology, Psychology, and Societal Structures

Erik Erikson, a celebrated psychologist from the twentieth century, developed what became one of the most popular and influential theories of development. His theory centered on the psychosocial development of individuals. Erikson said that life as the individual experiences it is produced by the interaction and modification of three major systems: biological, psychological, and societal.[3] All three systems can be modified by an individual's choices, but the integration and interaction of these systems shape human thought and behavior.

From a psychosocial perspective, development is derived from the constant interaction of the individual and their social

---

[3] Erik H. Erikson, *The Life Cycle Completed: A Review.*

environment. At each stage, people dedicate a lot of energy and time to become skilled at psychological tasks that they need to adapt to their society. Each stage presents what is known as a new *normative crisis*. This is a crisis arising from internal conflicts associated with each stage because there is a tension between a person's abilities and new demands from their social group. To reduce the tension, people not only use coping mechanisms that they already know but also develop new ways to cope.

Once a crisis has to be faced, there will be a resolution, which can go in two directions. If there is a positive resolution, the individual will develop new skills and learn how to adapt and resolve the new challenges based on a better understanding of themself and others. A negative resolution will create rigidity, leading the individual to become defensive or withdraw entirely. This will have a detrimental impact on a person's ability to adapt in subsequent stages.

In the psychosocial perspective, the dynamics between self and others is highly important. It is based on this dynamic of interpersonal relationships, as well as the dynamics of interaction between the three systems (biological, psychological, and societal) that meaning is created. A strong component of making meaning is the emergence of one's identity. Each stage will provide new challenges that contribute to uncovering and redefining one's identity.

As an investor moves through the stages of investing development, they will be challenged by deciding what type of investor they are. This means they'll need to sort out what level of risk they can take, what type of investment they prefer, how involved they want to be in the management of their investment, and many other questions that will keep emerging and pushing them into developing an identity and maturity.

Growth will come from learning, which in turn comes from the interaction of individual and social interactions, and the dynamics between the three systems (biological, physiological, and societal). A description of each of the three structures follows, outlining what each structure entails and how they each impact on an investor's development.

The biological system

The *biological system* refers to all bodily functions and processes required for an organism to function. The main focus for the purpose of this book is on the mind, mental processes, and the mind's evolutionary path to maturation. Maturation for biological processes is directed mainly by genetics but also by the influence of the environment and the resources available, such as nutrition, air quality, and even sunlight. Other aspects that can have an impact are exposure to diseases or accidents that occur while an organism is growing up.

Lifestyle choices such as diet, exercise, sleep patterns, stress, or drug use will have an impact on mental processes and decision-making. As mentioned before, these are all aspects that are choices an individual can make. That means that instead of these aspects being dependent on genetics, they are dependent on the person. A person has power and control over their choices. And those choices will have an impact on the biological system.

Maturity of the biological system will happen because of the lapse of time, and the changes of the system will be driven by genetics. Health and longevity are fields of study in themselves, but whatever new findings science reaches, the fact remains that time has an effect on biology. The changes that happen to the system will affect mind processes, therefore influencing investment choices for an investor.

The psychological system

The *psychological system* relates to mental processes, which include processing information, memory, emotions, language, perception, cognitive and affective cycles, problem-solving, etc. The psychological system provides the resources to navigate reality, helping us to make meaning of a situation and have an orientation to the future.

Just like the biological system, the psychological system changes over time. While some of the change is driven by genetics, a significant part is developed through accumulated experience. The same can be said for the capacity for intellectual functioning; intelligence and cognitive capacity are based on genetics and nurtured or subdued by environmental stimuli.

Lev Vygotsky, a twentieth-century psychologist known for his work on psychological development in children, thought that psychological tools mediate mental processes.[4] People are not born with such tools—the tools are acquired through life experience and need to be mastered. Language, concepts, signs, and symbols were the main psychological tools Vygotsky thought people used for higher mental processes. Those tools are what distinguish a young child and an animal with basic instincts and lower psychological functioning from a more mature or psychologically evolved person.

The societal system

The *societal system* is integrated mostly through interpersonal relationships, but it spans to a macroscopic level as well. Family, culture, politics, religious ideologies, economic patterns, exposure to racism or other forms of intergroup hostility, and war and peace have an impact on the psychosocial development of a person. However, the highest impact the societal system has on the psychosocial development of an individual is significant or close interpersonal relationships.

The closest relationship the average individual has is with their family. First with their family of origin and in later stages of life, with the family they form. Because humans are social animals,

---

[4] Lev Vygotsky, *Mind in Society: The Development of Higher Psychological Processes.*

everyone has a family and social circle they participate in. A *family* can be defined as a group that has bonds through blood relation, people who cohabitate, or people who are connected through emotional ties. While the concept of family is continually redefined because of cultural and/or political changes, how a person is socialized in the earlier stages of life will have the most impact on their worldview and the way they relate to others. Family influence is constantly present but will evolve continuously.

Another big factor in the societal system is culture. *Culture* is a set of rules that guides how people in a group relate or interact with each other, and it determines a significant part of a person's worldview. It defines how people see themselves in relation to their environment and others, strongly influencing their understanding of reality. But most importantly, culture is a huge component in how people think and how they make decisions. While investors strive to make rational decisions, their decisions are always biased and filtered through their worldviews, culture and, most of all, family history.

Finally, it is important to mention that, just like the other two systems, societal processes also change over time. A person who relates to others takes on a social role, and such roles can and will shift in a lifespan. Taking on new roles brings on new demands for a person. Those new demands in turn bring about new behaviors because people will be dealing with new or different expectations from others.

Main Concepts of the Developmental Perspective

Life span

A developmental perspective requires analyzing the life span and life's different periods. This book applies the developmental perspective to analyze an investor's journey. Some topics that can be explored through the developmental perspective are: How long does it take to become a mature investor who is confident in their investment decisions? When can someone become an investor? How long can a person be an investor? Most of the answers to these questions come from an understanding of the combination of factors involved in each of the three main systems: the biological, psychological, and societal.

Life expectancy plays a role in the life span and the stages an investor goes through. That's because one of the most important factors in any kind of investment is time. Projections of life expectancy can help provide a timeline that a person can be an investor. Several research institutions provide statistics with an average life expectancy of seventy-five years for males and eighty years for females. Again, this is a simple average based on several organizations' projections, and these numbers tend to change as scientific discoveries progress.

Beyond scientific discoveries, there are many other factors involved in longevity. The factor of education has consistently been found to increase the life expectancy of people across many societies. The more years of education, the longer the life expectancy. This and the other factors form a timeframe an investor has to traverse the stages and see their investments perform.

While it is rare to see a ten-year-old become an investor, there is always an outlier who will have much more time in their investment career. An outlier can also be found in the opposite direction. For instance, an individual who makes a first investment in their seventies. Such a person will naturally have less time to tackle the learning curve and move through the stages of an investor's life cycle. Yet most importantly the factor of time affecting their investments will be significantly reduced.

Stages of development

A *stage of development* is a period of life with particular characteristics distinguishing the stage from the previous and/or the next stage. Each stage presents new and unique challenges that will lead people to attain new skills. The development of said new skills or lack of them may explain some individuals' behaviors. For example, in earlier stages of life a person is concerned with earning their parents' approval. Then later on a person is focused on being accepted or even recognized by their peers. Even further along, a person seeks to understand themself.

There are different classic theories that discuss stages of life, such as Sigmund Freud's psychosexual theory of development or Jean Piaget's cognitive stages of development that establish ages for each stage; both set clear normative expectations for people's development. Erikson's psychosocial theory is not so concerned with an exact timeframe for each stage. Instead, he believed that each person is unique and will navigate the stages at their own rhythm. This book uses a similar approach because the investing life cycle has a different start for each investor and the expectations can be distinct.

Psychosocial theory is preoccupied with growth and psychological and social development of a human being, thus creating a universal theory that applies to every person. While any baby who is born will navigate the stages of development through the scope of their own family and culture, the developmental tasks for anyone will be the same. And no one has any kind of head start to get through the challenges. An investor's journey differs slightly because while the stages of development are universal, people do come from different backgrounds. Their families, cultures, education, age, and other factors are distinct and will have an effect on how a person navigates their development as an investor.

Let's consider a man who becomes an investor at forty years old. He was born to an affluent family and has heard about family investments, money managers, the stock market, commercial real estate, etc. his whole life. He will probably integrate the skills required to be an investor in a natural fashion. In addition to applying this innate skillset, he will probably have lots of support along the way. That could include cognitive or knowledge-based sponsorship, emotional support, help with investing networks, and maybe even financial backing. This may sound ideal, but there are disadvantages to such a situation as well, such as the enormous pressure created by social expectations.

Compare the previous situation to a man born to lower socioeconomic status in a country with an emerging economy. He is incredibly bright and manages to immigrate to an industrialized country where he becomes a successful executive in a large corporation. He generates good income, and with the surplus of money he has, he wants to make an investment that will provide income to help his family. Navigating the investor's development stages can seem much more overwhelming for him. Even though he is a bright and capable person, he might not have the same emotional sustenance to occupy the role of investor. Therefore, he might need more time, energy, or support to transition through the developmental stages.

Strengths come from successful resolution of conflicts at every stage. Going back to a previous stage is not possible because the experience has been accumulated, but a person can review and reframe a previous stage through the scope of newly acquired experiences. In fact, a person can encounter a theme from a previous stage and see it in a new light, and this occurs frequently. That could happen because they've added to their skills, and because of that, they can reinterpret the situation and make new meaning of past experiences.

Finally, it's important to note there are clearly defined, progressive stages, and the challenges for each one must be overcome to develop the skills of each stage. Yet it's common to see people anticipate later challenges before they are actually at a given maturity level. This could happen with someone who wants to become a gold investor and is running due diligence on a significant investment in a mining company when the person barely just bought their first few gold coins. They are anticipating the issues that are situated far ahead. The experience of having made a first investment raises awareness of issues that will come up when a significant investment takes place, even if that will not happen for a long time. But to be successful, an investor needs to mature and develop the required skills to move into more significant investments.

Tasks

Robert Havighurst introduced the concept of developmental tasks in the fifties.[5] He believed that development is a process in which people try to learn the goals assigned to them by the society they are trying to adapt to. The tasks change with age because expectations vary according to the individual's age. When someone achieves a task or learns well, they receive satisfaction and rewards. When a person does not learn well, they receive social disapproval, which can lead to suffering and negatively impact their self-esteem and/or self-concept.

One important concept Havighurst believed in was the *sensitive periods*. These are specific times when a person is most ready to learn a new skill, and he called them "teachable moments."[6] While he was mostly focused on the social expectations and impact on a person's development, he didn't completely discard the importance of biological maturation. He discussed these "teachable moments" periods from the perspective of a child growing up and acquiring life skills, but these periods happen when adults are trying to learn new abilities too. Most people learn skills in an order that is predetermined by the social group in which they live. If a particular task has not reached in the sensitive period, it will be much more difficult to learn later on.

Havighurst, Erikson, Freud, and many other scholars established different systems of stages with specific tasks to be

---

[5] Robert J. Havighurst, *Developmental Tasks and Education.*
[6] Robert J. Havighurst, *Human Development and Education.*

achieved in each stage. There are similarities and differences in their theories mostly because of the culture in which each scholar was embedded. Yet there are some essential components of what a *developmental task* means, regardless. The basics are that a person's problem-solving efforts and learning during any given specific stage are dominated by psychosocial challenges. As tasks are achieved, the person's abilities to participate in more complex social relationships, as well as their capacity for more complex problem-solving faculties, are improved.

Tasks are embedded in cultures because it is the culture that determines normative social standards for each individual. Cultures that persist through time have developed systems of teaching in which some behaviors are stimulated to help their members learn what they need to know at specific times. In an unconscious, primitive, and collective way, those specific behaviors are encouraged because the individual's survival, as well the group's, depend on them learning well.

Investors teach other aspiring investors their abilities because that is the way for them to perpetuate economic trade as they know it. While it may seem counterintuitive that an experienced investor will teach someone who eventually might become their competitor, they need to keep the investing culture alive by training new members and ushering them into the culture.

Psychosocial crisis

The concept of a psychosocial crisis comes from Erikson's 1963 theory. He believed a *psychosocial crisis* happens when an individual has to adapt to external demands of the social environment, which is something that happens at each stage of development.[7] People fall into crisis because of dealing with psychological stresses that are a

---

[7] Erik H. Erikson, *Childhood and Society.*

normal set of strains; it doesn't have to be an extraordinary event that thrusts someone into a psychosocial crisis.

A state of tension is created before the end of any given stage that derives not only from an individual trying to achieve a resolution for society's demands but also from transforming those demands into personal interpretations. What people are trying to do is reduce the tension. Once they are able to find a way to do it, they can move on to the next stage.

Every time there is a crisis it's because people are being faced with the current developmental task. The ability to master such challenges will be influenced by how the tasks were accomplished in the prior stages. The resolution of the crisis will lead to the development of new abilities. It will have a strong impact on a person's self-esteem and will help orient an individual toward the future.

The chances of a completely positive or completely negative resolution are small. Most people will usually achieve a task resolution that will fall somewhere along the spectrum between extremely positive to extremely negative. However, as the stages progress, the probability increases for a resolution falling more and more on the negative side. That is because the tasks become increasingly complex and the obstacles to developmental growth multiply.

At every stage there is a constant tension that generates a dynamic between the positive and the negative poles of the possibilities of resolving the stressful situation of meeting societal demands. The dynamics created by such tension contribute to moving a person to experience different perspectives of life; this propels them to develop new abilities, constantly widening the range of a person's adaptive capabilities. Based on this concept, this book uses the term *investment crisis* to describe the two opposing poles that create the dynamic of a crisis an investor will face in each stage.

Coping mechanisms

In psychosocial theory, coping behavior refers to consciously trying to adapt to stressful situations. To cope, people start with an appraisal of the situation, considering the many factors that can be influencing the stress they're encountering. The next step is to assess and decide which cognitive, affective, or behavioral strategies need to be applied to manage the stress that was produced.

Erikson thought a positive resolution of a psychosocial crisis of any given stage would develop what he called *prime adaptive ego qualities*.[8] These are resources that help someone cope when they face a crisis. Erikson described these ego qualities as mental states that orient a person in their interpretation of life experiences. While these ego qualities contribute significantly to a person's worldview, they are constantly restructured to add new qualities. Erikson may have introduced this concept in his writings, but it has since been validated by research.

Just like people need to develop their prime adaptive ego qualities to better adapt to life situations, investors need to develop what I have deemed *"investor adaptive qualities."* These qualities are the strengths that will contribute to the constant evolution of a person's investment thesis and investing abilities.

Finally, an important quality to note is hope. Erikson found that people who were hopeful about their own futures and those of their families were more intellectually strong and psychologically resilient than people with negative attitudes. People with a hopeful attitude had a better chance of holding up when faced with crisis. The ego strength quality of hope has been found to be a strong predictor in life satisfaction.

Having reviewed all the main concepts from psychosocial theory, the next step is to bring them all into context in the investing world. The coming chapters present an application of psychosocial theory's main concepts to describe the life cycle of an investor. Each of the following chapters describes a stage of an investor's development, improving our understanding of what a person must learn to become a mature investor.

---

[8] Erik H. Erikson, *Adulthood*.

CHAPTER 3

Stage 1: Ingenuous Impetus

Developmental Tasks:
1. **Maturation of understanding the basics of investing**
2. **Developing respect for the risks involved**
3. **Emotional development**

Investment Crisis: Fearful versus imprudent

Central Process: Replication

Investor Adaptive Quality: Hope

Core Issue: Dropping out as an investor

I called the first stage in the development of an investor *ingenuous impetus* because when someone actually decides to start investing, they come into the investing world with a naïveté of what they will actually be running into but with high emotions about the matter. The emotions felt by the novice investor will range between being fearful about making their first investments to being overexcited and imprudent because they don't understand the risks involved. That is the spectrum of forces that generates the dynamic of the fearful versus imprudent investment crisis.

This first stage is a time of tremendous growth. Going from zero to one investment is an infinitesimal change in experience, from one to two is a 100% change again, and even with a third investment the change is still a 33%. Any seasoned investor would be delighted to have double-digit returns on any investment any time, let alone triple digits. An infinitesimal gain in an investment? Mathematically impossible when talking about investing assets, but it is not impossible when the gain is personal development.

That first investment is the equivalent of a baby making their first coordinated moves or saying their first words. After the baby starts babbling, it's soon followed by grabbing, talking, and walking. But those first attempts seem clumsy, cute, and funny to an observing adult. With time, practice, and proper guidance, the baby will learn how to talk and walk well. Similarly, with such practice and support, a novice investor will acquire focus, become more tempered, and increase intuition on what can be a good investment.

To become a better investor, a person will have to go through one of the major changes that happen in the ingenuous impetus stage. They'll have to start taking action toward their investment goals. Ideally within this stage, an investor will also move from simply responding to what they deem to be an opportunity in making an investment to having a more controlled, planned, and proactive approach to investing.

Developmental Tasks

Maturation of understanding the basics of investing

While the developmental path to becoming a seasoned investor is the same for everyone, people who become investors have different backgrounds, ages, business experience, or areas of expertise. Someone with a background in accounting is more likely to feel more comfortable with becoming an investor than someone who has experience as a school teacher. Nevertheless, both example investors need to get better acquainted with the basics of investing, or perhaps review the former obtained knowledge in new light and with new goals in mind.

Learning the basics of investing is like learning a language. In fact, it is very similar to when a toddler develops communication skills. Children acquire communicative competence when they know how to use all the aspects in language that enables them to effectively participate in social interactions. Psychosocial development begins with human interaction, which is almost entirely dependent on communication skills. An investor's development begins when they start to become familiar with investment concepts and language.

It is not uncommon for a beginning investor to feel quickly overwhelmed when they start to hear terms such as trading on *margin*, *shorting a stock*, or the *P/E ratio* of a company's stock. Even simple concepts such as how to calculate *return on investment (ROI)* and how that differs from the *internal rate of return (IRR)* can be daunting. Understanding these and other key concepts helps the investor develop language about investing. As the knowledge base grows and these concepts are actually used in real investments, the terms will be added to the language naturally. Then the person internalizing these concepts will feel more and more comfortable with the terms.

Becoming comfortable with these new terms is one important sign that a person is moving forward in their investment journey. On a biological level, these adjustments demonstrate *neural plasticity*, which are changes in the interconnections of the brain's neurons that derive from new learning and experience. The vast knowledge and range of experiences a human can go through are impossible to anticipate. The human brain is designed to take in new information and use it to guide thoughts and actions for which new neural pathways are developed and strengthened.

During the first three years of life, a human brain grows three times in weight and creates over a trillion connections among the neurons. Becoming an investor is something that for the great majority of people happens when they are adults, so their brains will not change as much as a baby's brain. Nevertheless, many new neural pathways must be developed for the investor to act in their new role. New knowledge will stimulate the growth, and experience will reinforce the new pathways.

Developing respect for the risks involved

The dynamic of this stage stems from the movement between the opposing poles of being too afraid of making an investment and being imprudent about investing. Imprudence usually comes because of a fantasy that almost any investment will yield positive results. A novice investor will typically come into their first investments with a stronger inclination toward one side or the other. The reasons for their initial approach lie in their personal history, but regardless of their inclination, every young investor needs to find a way to find balance among such tension.

For young investors seeking this balance during the ingenuous impetus stage, it's important to master one key component—learning respect for the risks involved in investing. Some expert investors are very focused on risk management, and even after they have gained vast experience and success, they dedicate a significant amount of time to risk control.

Respect does not mean being afraid, neither does it mean simply acknowledging the existence of risk. Developing respect means considering that any investment involves taking a risk. There are many variables that should be considered when taking a risk. They include awareness of the risks involved, risk management, risk aversion or tolerance, and perhaps most importantly, the emotions brought up by being exposed to risk.

Maturity as an investor will come, in part, from emotional maturity. Emotional maturity can be stimulated through self-knowledge and increased awareness of one's own reactions and tendencies. As an investor, it would be especially important to know one's tendencies when they must deal with risk. The higher the awareness or degree of consciousness about one's own reactions, the easier it is to manage the risk faced. Once an investor heightens their level of respect for risk, they will be moving in the direction of making more rational investment decisions.

A note on rationality: My personal stance is that rational decisions should never be a goal. Rational decision-making is a topic continuously mentioned in the business/financial literature, but I think it is impossible to make what would be deemed a truly rational decision. So no one should stress about such a thing. The reason I believe it's impossible is because economists believe a rational decision is, very simply put, choosing what you like best.[9] However, there are numerous psychological explanations and social psychology experiments that demonstrate that what is psychologically rational can be the opposite of what would be considered economically rational.[10]

One of the reasons for such disparity, according to Freud, is that people must limit their pleasure seeking in order to relate to society.[11] So early on in their lives, people internalize a series of restrictions that will constrain their choices, so their behavior might be "economically irrational" while making sense internally. Sometimes a choice can actually make sense from many perspectives, but it depends on too many factors.

This is a controversial matter in the field of behavioral economics and not the subject matter of this book. But it's important to note because keeping in mind that there are no decisions that are 100% rational when making investments should be a relief to novice investors. Especially those who might have the mindset of "What is the best decision?"

It is easy to categorize a decision as being rational or not when looking in hindsight, but it is impossible to make a rational decision

---

[9] James Campbell, "What an Economist Means by Rationality."
[10] Debra Friedman and Barry R. Weingast, "Rational Choice and Freudian Accounts of Cooperation."
[11] Sigmund Freud, "Civilization and its Discontents."

at the time the process is happening. The goal should be to master the tasks in the developmental stages, evolve as an investor, and have a keener intuition about how to move forward.

Humans are irrational beings, and it has been proven many times over. We can look to Apple for an example. When Apple first released their iconic iPhone, no one had ever seen such a piece of technology before. They were introducing a breakthrough in technology to the world. When the iPhone became available in the stores, it had a price of $599 USD, but only two months later in what almost seemed to be a social psychology or behavioral economics experiment, they dropped the price to $399 USD.

As soon as the price dropped, there were lines of people camping outside of the Apple stores begging to get an iPhone. It only seemed to make sense to want an iPhone when they had been "reduced in price." It seems like a rational decision, except for the fact that the average price of a cell phone in 2008 when the iPhone was released was $140 USD. Since there was no benchmark to the iPhone and people had no way to assign a value to the new trendy gadget, Apple created the illusion that they had overpriced their new device and $399 USD was the new fair value. People responded by flocking into the stores and buying millions upon millions of iPhones across the world. The truth is that at $399 USD, the iPhone was the one of the most expensive cell phones or personal tech gadgets the world had ever seen.

Emotional development

As has been mentioned, an essential aspect to finding balance in this stage's crisis is emotional development. One of the most significant effects of the crisis from the push-pull of being fearful or imprudent is the emotional agitation that a beginner investor will experience when trying to decide whether to get involved in an investment or not.

Emotional maturity is something to strive for throughout a lifetime. It is a process integrated by many components that yields a generalized attitude and worldview. As an investor, the development of a more mature way to manage the emotions that arise from considering a new investment, or even managing one, is crucial to enhancing the investor's abilities.

For a few decades, the field of behavioral economics has been studying how emotions shape decisions that involve making a choice to maximize what they call utility. *Utility* means the desirability of an outcome. However, economists and psychologists who are interested in decision-making processes have noticed something recently. They've learned that people's choices are more influenced by their immediate emotions than by the consequences of their choices.

A significant interest in the field of behavioral economics is the area of decision-making when encountering risk. Any investor making a decision is facing a risk because there are no guaranties of the outcome. The emotional experience people have in the moment they are making a decision is completely cognitive. People are trying to forecast how they would feel if the investment goes one way or another, which will have an important influence on making a choice. Yet there's evidence that people have difficulty making such predictions.[12]

Scott Rick and George Lowenstein, professors and researchers who specialize in social and decision sciences, explain that in some cases, immediate emotions, which arise from contemplating the potential outcomes of a decision, can play a beneficial role in the

---

[12] Philip Brickman et al., "Lottery Winners and Accident Victims: Is Happiness Relative?," *Journal of Personality and Social Psychology*; George Loewenstein and Daniel Adler, "A Bias in the Prediction of Tastes," *The Economic Journal*; Deborah A. Kermer et al., "Loss Aversion Is an Affective Forecasting Error," *Psychological Science*; Michael Conlin et al., "Projection Bias in Catalog Orders," *American Economic Review*.

decision-making process.[13] One reason for this is that the contemplation process can inform the person of their own values, helping the person steer in a direction that will prove satisfactory because they are following their personal convictions. This may very well prove to be true with an investor who makes the choice of investing in a company that claims to hold a philosophy aligned with the person's personal beliefs. The investor will likely be satisfied with such investment even if the return on the investment is somewhat lower than what they could have made had they made a different choice.

Clarifying personal values and beliefs and knowing how to apply them when making investments is a sign of maturity as an investor, but emotional development also happens at the biological level. Neuroscientists now have abundant technology and have completed plenty of studies that have improved our understanding about the neurophysiology of emotions and behaviors, particularly when it comes to fear. Some of these studies inform the development of the stage of ingenuous impetus crisis and validate the important role of emotional development in a person becoming a successful investor.

Investment Crisis: Fearful vs. Imprudent

Fear and lack thereof are the emotions governing the developmental task and the investment crisis of this stage. Without going into too much detail of the neurophysiology of emotions, many studies have found that the amygdala plays an important role in the assignment of affective significance to events perceived through sensory stimuli.

The *amygdala* is a part of the brain that is somewhat of an alarm system. It reacts when it interprets a situation as a threat, and

---

[13] Scott Rick and George Lowenstein, "The Role of Emotion in Economic Behavior," in *Handbook of Emotions.*

these types of fear reactions tend to be consistent. This of course has obvious evolutionary survival advantages as it has enabled the species to stay alive because they are keeping records of previously encountered dangerous situations. That recordkeeping and recall allows us to respond quickly to similar circumstances.

At a purely psychological level, the inability to prevent fear responses can carry significant problems. Someone who cannot control fear responses can suffer from a severe anxiety disorder such as generalized anxiety disorder, post-traumatic stress disorder, phobias, etc. As an investor, someone with the inability to counter-balance fear will be permanently paralyzed; they probably won't ever be able to make an investment. That's in extreme and rare cases, of course.

Yet it's also possible to learn that a certain stimulus does not pose a danger anymore, therefore allowing us to react in a way other than a response to fear. There are a number of studies that show that the medial prefrontal cortex is involved, not only in regulating the amygdala but also in the extinction process of the reactions to fear.[14] The *prefrontal cortex* is the part of the brain that is involved in executive function, which means it takes part in things like planning, decision-making, problem-solving, and self-control.

The aforementioned studies suggest that people have unique cognitive means to control fear responses. These mechanisms that are exclusive to humans are the instruments that can provide the emotional maturity an investor needs, and the main components that can stimulate this emotional evolution are education and

---

[14] Maria A. Morgan et al., "Extinction of Emotional Learning: Contribution of Medial Prefrontal Cortex," *Neuroscience Letters*; Maria A. Morgan and Joseph E. LeDoux, "Differential Contribution of Dorsal and Ventral Medial Prefrontal Cortex to the Acquisition and Extinction of Conditioned Fear in Rats," *Behavioral Neuroscience*; Gregory J. Quirk et al., "The Role of Ventromedial Prefrontal Cortex in the Recovery of Extinguished Fear," *Journal of Neuroscience*; Mohammed R. Milad and Gregory J. Quirk, "Neurons in Medial Prefrontal Cortex Signal Memory for Fear Extinction," *Nature*; Gregory J. Quirk et al., "Prefrontal Mechanisms in Extinction of Conditioned Fear," *Biological Psychiatry*.

experience. The former is easily attained through an infinite number of options in investment education, while the latter requires that the individual takes a leap, which can be daunting.

One way to resolve the fear of getting started and what can help balance this stage's opposing poles is the central process of replication.

Central Process: Replication

One way in which a novice investor can feel much more secure in getting started is by having someone who provides support. A teacher, a mentor, an investor's club, a subscription service, taking a course—something that can provide the new investor with enough certainty to move them in the direction of getting started.

Replicating investing behaviors of more seasoned investors is just like being a toddler when the main way of learning is imitating others. Imitation is always a great way of learning, especially when starting anything new. Toddlers imitate their parents and while they are emulating the observed behaviors, reactions, and attitudes, toddlers are also internalizing what they are copying and making these behaviors their own.

Toddlers have no sense whatsoever of social norms or expectations, so they are completely free and have no standards to conform to; this enables them to simply imitate what they see with no sense of what it means. In other words, they don't fear judgment or shame. An adult observer finds these imitation games funny and cute precisely because the toddler has no idea what they are doing and/or because the observer can see the toddler acting just like their parent. But once the toddler makes these behaviors their own, they are theirs to use at will or, as the toddler matures, to analyze and modify their behaviors that they deem worthwhile.

Replication is the central process of the ingenuous impetus stage because few things can help a beginner investor feel more secure than the feeling of not being alone in a new endeavor, especially one that involves taking serious risks. Any investor is always risking financial assets, but they are also risking, among other things, their self-esteem being damaged. A beginner needs to create a solid base of knowledge and positive experience to propel their investing journey forward. Following a trustworthy example can be incredibly comforting.

The dynamic that creates the momentum for a potential investor to move into the developmental journey starts in the ingenuous impetus stage because of the tensions created by the opposing forces of the investment crisis, which in this case are being too fearful versus being imprudent. This tension will create movement, which is necessary, but it's also crucial to find a balance and a mechanism that will help resolve the tension. When the balance is found, the individual will find themself in a position of having obtained knowledge and experience as well as increased maturity.

Investor Adaptive Quality: Hope

When the investment crisis is effectively resolved, the investor will achieve a new adaptive quality, which in this stage is hope. *Hope* comes from the understanding of the self as a causal agent of the positive resolution of the crisis. Hopefulness combines the ability to think of one or more paths to achieve a goal with a belief in one's ability to move along that pathway toward the goal.[15]

While hope is an expectation of positive outcomes, research suggests that people with optimistic perspectives of the future usually have higher levels of confidence that their goals will be reached. That in turn creates greater persistence when facing obstacles, which leads to higher levels of performance.[16] Barbara

---

[15] Charles R. Snyder et al., "Hope: An Individual Motive for Social Commerce," *Group Dynamics: Theory, Research, and Practice.*
[16] Charles R. Snyder, "Hope Theory: Rainbows in the Mind," *Psychological Inquiry.*

Newman and Philip Newman, two well-known developmental psychologists, believe that people who have higher levels of hopefulness undertake a larger number of goals across life areas and select tasks that are more difficult.[17]

As an investor, being able to tolerate uncertainty is imperative. No one knows what the future holds, but there is only one thing that is guaranteed: The world is always changing. Changes can occur at a more accelerated rate at times, while in other times we have periods of stability. But there is always a certain amount of doubt about what will happen when starting a new endeavor.

That is why hope is an essential quality an investor needs to develop. Someone with no hope will never be able to move out of the state of being too fearful to make an investment. And an individual who is too hopeful will likely not do enough due diligence before undertaking an investment. There needs to be just enough hope that will push a person to be persistent in working toward their goal with a sense of assurance that things will work out well. But there has to be enough skepticism that they will be thorough in their due diligence work before committing assets into an investment.

Core Issue: Dropping Out as an Investor

If the crisis for the ingenuous impetus stage subdues the investor's adaptive qualities, then the core issue will prevail. That means that the tasks and abilities that the investor needed to develop in the stage or the goals for the stage were not met, and the investor's maturity was not enhanced.

In this stage the core issue, which is the worst-case scenario, would be that the potential investor stops and throws away their intention of becoming an investor. It is very sad to see that a

---

[17] Barbara M. Newman and Philip R. Newman, *Development through Life: A Psychosocial Approach.*

potential investor drops out of the race at a time when the typical behavior should be characterized by interest in the newness of the investing world, the delight of learning something new, and the thrill of actually making a first investment.

Potential investors who are characterized by the core issue of dropping out usually seem passive, even lethargic about their potential projects and have neutral or negative affective behavior toward the investments they are considering. Some variables that can contribute to an investor falling for the core issue can be the individual's temperament. For example, someone with an anxious-avoidant attachment style will have a higher probability of dropping out as an investor.

Attachment theory is a psychological theory that helps us understand people's personalities and ways they relate with others; it is particularly focused on early development and how that impacts people's style of relating to others as adults.[18] While psychologists tend to think of the attachment styles as ways in which individuals relate to each other, there are other relationships people establish in life, such as an investment. While an investment in no way can substitute nor provide what a relationship with another person delivers, there are many parallels between an interpersonal relationship and participating in an investment. As such, the investor's personality and personal history will have a strong component in how an investment is handled.

The anxious-avoidant attachment style main traits include: worrying about rejection, feeling uncomfortable with closeness in relationships, a higher risk of social anxiety and depression, as well as less-fulfilling interpersonal relationships. Anxiously attached individuals want to rely on others but worry they won't be equally reciprocated. They want to have a close relationship but feel uncomfortable relying on others.

---

[18] Jude Cassidy, "The Nature of a Child's Ties," in *Handbook of Attachment: Theory, Research, and Clinical Applications*.

Fortunately recent research suggests that attachment styles can be changed.[19] In general, what the literature suggests is that attachment styles can change through psychotherapy but also that an insecurely/anxious/avoidant attached individual can greatly improve from being in a relationship with a more securely attached person. So the central process for this stage, which is replication, can greatly help a potential investor become more secure. Also, replication can help an investor become a more securely attached individual who will greatly increase their odds of having not only better investments but also better relationships. And that contributes to an overall happier, better adapted, and more fulfilling life.

---

[19] Meghan Laslocky, "How to Stop Attachment Insecurity from Ruining Your Love Life," *Greater Good Magazine*; Barbara Murphy and Glen W. Bates, "Adult Attachment Style and Vulnerability to Depression," *Personality and Individual Differences*; Hal Shorey, "Come Here, Go Away: The Dynamics of Fearful Attachment," *Psychology Today*.

CASE STUDY 1
Oliver's Yearning

When Oliver was twenty-nine years old, he felt he needed a change. He had been working for a large corporation for some time, and while he was doing a good job and was appreciated at his office, he was not really feeling satisfied with his current work nor his income. Oliver yearned for more. He had a lot of interests and aspirations but thought he was at a standstill and felt trapped. He was miserably uncertain about what to do with his life in general, but he just kept going.

Oliver grew up in a family that had significant economic ups and downs. He watched his father climb the corporate ladder for years and become really successful. Oliver's father had been able to provide increasingly more for his family as Oliver and his younger brother were growing up. The family went from living in a tiny apartment (in a not-so-great part of the city) to living in a large house in a gated community in one of the best parts of the city. Their vacation trips kept getting fancier, their cars kept being upgraded, and Oliver just kept getting more and more things. Further down the line, his parents decided to buy a vacation house at a prominent ski resort and join a renowned country club.

When the family moved to their new house, Oliver and his brother were transferred from the little school they were attending at the time to an upscale private school. All the kids in the new school were children of well-known businesspeople—top executives of multinational corporations or important politicians. While it was somewhat intimidating at first, Oliver and his brother adapted well to their new environment. They did well academically and developed close friends, even keeping in touch in the years after school.

When Oliver was in high school, his father decided to quit his job and start his own business. His father's plan was to capitalize on years of experience to build something of his own, just as he had seen many others do. He was going to use all his professional network and particular expertise to make a lot more money while cutting back on his work hours at the same time. At the beginning things were going great, but then a recession hit. The business suffered significantly.

After that the business was low on cash and high on debt. Oliver's father had overestimated his business's potential and overextended the risks he took. Perhaps a casualty of an overinflated ego, Oliver's father had a poorly positioned business in a time of high uncertainty. The business took a tremendous hit and went under. The material goods lost were astonishing, but the emotional cost was immeasurable.

Oliver's father spent years trying to pay off his debts and settle the lawsuits he was served with. He became an alcoholic and lost everything he owned. But he did manage to keep a small apartment for his family to live in. Later on his wife divorced him, and he was mostly estranged from the family. He became severely depressed and never even tried to get a job nor start a new business again. He was hardly getting by day by day.

Oliver's mother got a job to support her kids, who by then were in college. Oliver got a part-time job as well and managed to finish his college degree. His brother was younger and wasn't too concerned with helping out the family. Oliver became ultra-responsible by being in charge of consoling his mother and solving issue after issue that they encountered through the years.

Oliver grew up to become a smart, strong, highly focused, and determined man. He became very conservative when it came to money matters, but he was ambitious and knew he often held back. Through his life experiences, he became highly adaptable and although he fondly remembers the family ski trips, international travels, and weekends in the country club, he didn't really need much in terms of material possessions, trips, or luxuries of any kind. He was a humble hard worker who really wanted to move forward in life and avoid his father's mistakes.

Oliver was the type of person his friends could always rely on. Not really the soul of the party, but always present and participating in social events with his friends and family. They all very much enjoyed having Oliver around. He was the kind of guy who drove home whoever had a drink too many. He had a few relationships and had been thinking he would like to have a family of his own, but at the same time the mere thought of having a family brought up substantial anxiety.

After college, Oliver got a job in a large multinational corporation where he had been doing well, earning several promotions in his first eight years. His boss appreciated his excellent strategic vision, drive, and pursuit of growth. Oliver, however, had been ambivalent for a while about moving on and starting something of his own. But given his family history, Oliver just could not commit to a decision. He also didn't really feel like starting a small business, which is the only thing he could think of and had resources for.

In the years Oliver had been at this company, he had seen a couple of waves of mass employee cutbacks, and he knew being out of the job could happen anytime to anyone. What he really wanted was to, at the very least, supplement his income and have something that could provide him with further security than just depending on his job. Oliver's coworker had recently opened a brokerage account and started doing some trading, which got Oliver curious about investing. Yet Oliver felt it was too much risk to simply start speculating with stocks, something he knew little about.

Being the smart and highly cautious fellow that he was, Oliver did some research and put together a list of books he decided he needed to read before committing to anything, let alone putting any money in. He also registered for a few online courses on investing, where he learned about some conferences he then attended in person. All of these events helped him meet other potential investors like him and allowed him to listen to great stories from more experienced investors as well.

A year went by, and Oliver was absorbing so much new knowledge. Because of his personal history, Oliver was still quite hesitant about actually investing in anything. He had a few ideas about the investments he would like to pursue, as well as what he felt was solid knowledge and information. But he was really concerned with not losing his hard-earned money that he'd finally started saving.

After much thinking and many discussions with his family and friends, Oliver decided to actually jump in and make his first investment. Oliver had been thinking about buying a house for a while and decided to go ahead with that plan. But instead of just buying his own place, he would do it as an investment through a method he had recently learned.

While he had several ideas, much of what Oliver had been researching and learning was on real estate investing. He felt real estate was a solid, conservative, and potentially profitable investment. Besides, he was getting ready to buy a property anyway, so he figured the worst that could happen was that he ended up living in the property. He finally decided to use a strategy called *house hacking* where he would buy a duplex, living on one side and renting the other.

Oliver asked around and did a lot of research to find a business-savvy Realtor, and then he finally found someone who was very helpful. Oliver received a list of over thirty properties that fit the description of what he was looking for. He proceeded to drive by them as well as run the numbers, which helped him reduce his options to four duplexes. Out of those four, Oliver was very enthusiastic about one of them, especially because he would be living there as well. But when he went out to see the place, he figured the renovation costs could end up being an extra 50% to the property cost. He was very disappointed and had to discard that option.

He then visited the other three options, decided on one, and made an offer. A few days later he learned someone else had bought the property right from under his feet. Terrible disenchantment again! Oliver was very frustrated and considered dropping the whole idea. Then he thought maybe investing this way was not for him after all. He felt that investing was proving to be much more difficult than he'd anticipated.

A couple weeks later, the Realtor called and said he just got notice of a property coming on the market and felt it would be perfect for Oliver. Oliver got really excited and asked for all the info. He liked everything about the property except that it came out at the top of his budget, which meant Oliver wouldn't have any money left for renovations. He went out to see the place and wasn't too happy about its aesthetics, but thought he could tolerate living in such conditions for some time while he had enough money to make the needed improvements. He was actually more concerned with being able to offer a decent place to rent so he could get as much income as possible.

A little hesitant, Oliver bought that duplex. Oliver was a handy guy so he fixed as much as he could by himself, saving on labor costs. He also asked a designer friend to help with some ideas to make the spaces as nice as possible on a super low budget. He was able to accomplish more than what he had imagined.

The plan paid off. Oliver did everything he had learned in all the books he had read, the courses he took, and the conferences he attended. He bought a duplex, made all the improvements he could to add value, and made it as nice as possible not only because he was going to be living there but also so he could get the other space rented quickly. He was lucky enough that as soon as he moved in, the other space got rented.

Oliver felt like he hit a home run! Even though he had been so hesitant, Oliver was incredibly happy about owning the space where he lived. He was even happier about the rent he was collecting, particularly because it was enough to be cashflow positive. That meant Oliver was collecting enough rent to pay for the mortgage and other expenses he had from owning the property and still had some cash left every month.

Oliver learned every investment carried a certain degree of risk but also that the only way to actually make a profit was by taking some risk. Oliver was not very comfortable taking risks, but at least this time he felt it paid off. He learned about due diligence for a real estate investment and increased his investing experience immeasurably. He went from dreaming about owning a house and increasing his income to becoming a property-owning investor.

From the time when Oliver started considering he wanted to increase his income to when he collected the first rent after moving to his new place, Oliver went through an emotional roller coaster. He experienced an immeasurable range of emotions. Oliver had wanted to increase his income and feel more secure but didn't have the slightest idea of how to get there, which made him feel despair. But that evolved into to the ecstatic sensation derived from accomplishing what he set himself up for. Chief to achieving his goal was that through his investment process, Oliver acquired a property, moved to a new house, and even increased his income. His younger self would deem all of those feats unbelievable, yet he accomplished them all.

Going through the process, Oliver expanded his knowledge, experience, and even wealth. But above all, he heightened his aware-ness an immeasurable amount when it came to how he thought, felt, and reacted to the many situations he'd encountered to find and execute his first investment. He now felt not only more secure about engaging in the investment process again but also certain he could become a successful investor.

Case Analysis of Stage 1: Ingenuous Impetus

In relation to the process a person should go through in the first stage of becoming an investor, we can analyze Oliver's story to understand his performance and progress. Through Oliver's background and actions taken this far, Oliver has achieved the following for the first stage, ingenuous impetus.

Developmental Tasks

1) **Maturation of understanding the basics of investing.** Oliver tended to be overly careful. He prepared as best as he could, and probably more than most people ever would, before moving forward with an investment. Oliver read books, took courses, attended conferences, talked to other investors, and probably felt like he needed to have all the knowledge in the world before risking a cent. Oliver was incredibly well-prepared to understand the basics of investments.

2) **Developing respect for the risks involved.** In Oliver's case, developing respect meant understanding the reality of the risks involved in investing. Oliver was so worried about risking anything and so concerned with not falling into the mistakes of his father, he had to learn that some degree of risk was necessary to be an investor. He did learn this lesson because he actually made an investment, and once he was successful with his plan, Oliver realized his fears were somewhat exaggerated and perhaps unfounded. Respecting risk meant being realistic.

3) **Emotional development.** Having struggled to make his first investment, Oliver finally realized he had been going through an intense emotional journey. But after he settled down from the cathartic state he got from his success, Oliver noticed how much he'd raised his awareness about how he handled everything. Then he was in a much better emotional shape to take on more investing.

Investment Crisis: Fearful vs. Imprudent

Oliver started his investment journey being notoriously fearful, which makes sense in light of his family history and personal background. Oliver went through the crisis because he could logically understand it was possible to make investments and actually make a profit, but unconsciously he had significant fear pulling him in the direction of inaction.

The crisis drove him to what is commonly known as *analysis paralysis*. Oliver spent at least a year reading and studying about investments before even deciding to get his feet wet. However, much to his credit, Oliver was able to resolve the crisis in a positive direction and make an investment.

Central Process: Replication

With Oliver being so concerned about not following in his father's footsteps, it was relatively easy for him to go out and look for reputable and sensible authors and teachers he could learn from. When Oliver finally decided to take action, he followed their suggestions exactly and, at least this time, he was successful.

By following along the lines of what he learned, Oliver managed to successfully make his first investment. But the true profit was that Oliver gained knowledge, experience and, most importantly, a tremendous amount of self-confidence. He needed to have a guide initially, but then he felt he could actually do it and do it well.

Investor Adaptive Quality: Hope

Having achieved the tasks and resolved the crisis in a positive direction, Oliver would move forward to the next stage with the investor's adaptive quality of hope. He achieved this quality because after doing everything he thought was necessary and effectively going through the central process of replication, he was now a lot more confident and optimistic.

Oliver developed a conscious sense of security based on his experience but also an unconscious feeling of belief in his abilities knowing he had the agency to propel forward a successful investment. Such a quality is the foundation of an active investor because no matter what they face in their path, they know they can always rely on their own abilities to positively resolve the issues encountered.

CHAPTER 4
Stage 2: Unfolding Acumen of Inquiry

Developmental Tasks:

1. Developing the investor's self-concept
2. Skill learning
3. Maturation of decision-making biases
4. A Sense of belonging to a peer group

Investment Crisis: Drive vs. Inadequacy

Central Process: Education

Investor Adaptive Quality: Proficiency

Core Issue: Idleness

In the second stage of an investor's life cycle, the individual is becoming an investor and taking on the role in a progressive fashion. Once a decision has been made about making one (or more than one) initial investment, the perspective will change and new abilities will be called upon.

While there is no set time for any of the stages, this second stage can be one of the longest because the tasks required can be demanding and time-consuming. The stage's processes can vary greatly from person to person, depending on how each individual decides to move forward in their investment journey. Yet everyone will have an array of options they will at least need to consider, and they'll have a great deal to learn. This stage is characterized by having an intense load of learning both in the personal realm as well as in the technical.

With the move from potential investor to being an investor, many possibilities open up. This can mean that choosing and pursuing a possibility requires a lot of energy, time, and dedication. In the unfolding acumen of inquiry stage the personal growth will happen in parallel with the technical learning, which is why the central process to resolve the conflict of the stage is *education*.

Throughout this stage of unfolding acumen of inquiry, the momentum is created by the crisis of the forces when the investor has a drive to push forward with the investments but feels inadequate with what they are doing. As the central process of getting educated unfolds, the investor should feel more secure in their decisions and hopefully will achieve the investor adaptive quality of *proficiency*.

A proficient investor has a clear picture of what type of investments are appealing to them, and they know how to find a potential investment. They also have the technical abilities to analyze a deal and likely have a team or group of peers they can relate to and count on as they choose their next step. But most importantly, the investor knows themself well, has a solid concept of themself as an investor, understands their limitations or risk aversity, and feels secure in their decision-making process.

If all the tasks for the stage of unfolding acumen of inquiry are not achieved, the investor risks developing *idleness*, which is the core issue for the stage. Being idle means the investor has become paralyzed and is simply not being able to move in any direction in their investment journey. This can happen for a number of reasons, all of which relate to not having achieved the tasks for the stage.

For example, one reason for someone to be idle is what's commonly referred to as analysis paralysis. In this case the investor might have found a potential investment, but it's possible the investment somewhat presented itself and the investor does not know if they are suitable for such opportunity. Perhaps the investment is in an industry unfamiliar to the investor, but they feel unsure about rejecting the opportunity.

Paralysis occurs because the investor is not yet ready to handle what is being presented. They may not have a clear concept of themself as an investor (see task 1 for this stage), so they are unsure of what type of investments align best with their goals. Or perhaps they do not yet have the necessary technical skills to analyze the investment (task 2). It could also be that they don't have a support network trustworthy enough to provide insight into the opportunity (task 4).

Becoming idle is an issue, but fortunately it can be prevented as well as resolved by achieving this stage's tasks. While the stage's crisis will happen and is required to create momentum, it can also be resolved through the main process of acquiring education. Ideally this helps the investor achieve a sense of proficiency so that they can move on to the next stage.

Developmental Tasks

There are four developmental tasks that need to be achieved in the stage of unfolding acumen of inquiry. Completing these tasks is necessary to positively resolve the stage's crisis.

Developing the investor's self-concept

The development of an individual's self-concept is at the very heart of the psychosocial theory, and it's deeply examined when the theory describes the development of a child. According to Epstein, the *self-concept* can be viewed as a theory that links the child's understanding of the nature of the world, the nature of the self, and the meaning of interactions between the two.[20] Equally important for a potential investor is the development of self-concept as an investor.

Children learn how to relate to the world based on the self-theory they develop, which is also informed by the reactions they receive from interactions with others. Investors learn about themselves and mature their self-concepts of being investors as they gain experience in relating themselves to the world of investing. Since the self-theory is based on personal experience and observations, the self-concept will be modified over time because of their changing abilities and emotional maturity.

The early development of a self-concept as an investor will typically start with the individual connecting their personal self-concept with their interest to become an investor. A self-concept as an investor will start to emerge from an individual evaluating potential investments as well as the suitability for their personality, interests, and goals. As the individual becomes involved in different types of investments, they can better gauge and define what type of investor they are.

Some elements that may define the self-concept of an investor are related to the type of investment a person likes, such as stocks and bonds or trading with art. Other examples of elements of the self-concept are the length of time an investor wants to hold their investment or the level of risk they can put up with. There are also many other nuances that define the self-concept.

The basic traits that every investor will need to define for themselves include risk tolerance, how active or passive they want to remain, their motivations for investing, and the degree of control over their investment they are comfortable with. These basic

---

[20] Seymour Epstein, "Cognitive-Experiential Self-Theory," in *Advanced Personality*; Seymour Epstein, "Cognitive-Experiential Self-Theory: An Integrative Theory of Personality," in *The Self with Others: Convergences in Psychoanalytic, Social, and Personality Psychology*; Seymour Epstein, "The Self-Concept Revisited: Or a Theory of a Theory," *American Psychologist*.

characteristics are critical in defining the investor's self-concept, which has significant impact on their investment journey. This understanding of self will also help the investor define what type of investments they should consider and which ones are simply not worth looking into.

Next, the investor must educate themself on the possibilities of investments available to them and decide what kind of investments they are interested in. Learning things such as whether they qualify as an accredited investor, a special status under financial regulations that provides access to complex and higher-risk investments. Such status is typically reserved for high-net-worth individuals, banks, financial institutions, and other large corporations. Not many novice investors will have access to such designation, but some might, and they will be able to invest in things such as venture capital, private equity, and hedge funds, and/or become angel investors. Even deciding their available capital for initial investment will further elucidate their self-concept, as well as clarify what type of investment they should look for.

Finally, to better define their identity, investors must decide specifics about the investments they would like to participate in, such as industry, private deals, or public markets, how their investments will be managed, etc. The goal of defining the self-concept/identity as an investor will help the individual easily identify investments opportunities that feel comfortable.

With the investment world being so vast, a clear self-concept means the investor has solid roots and develops a compass that can indicate the direction they should follow. Otherwise, the infinite investment options can disorient the investor and could prove to be very costly mistakes for the investor.

There are countless nuances to a self-concept, which experience further defines. For example, a novice investor who wants to become a real estate investor has many paths available to achieve this. Here are three examples of how investors define themselves as real estate investors, which also vary according to their level of expertise and the maturity of their self-concept:

1. I am a real estate investor. I bought an apartment that I rent and manage on my own.
2. I am a real estate investor. Since I am an accredited investor and a very busy person, I invest in a private, multifamily investment fund that's professionally managed and invests in the area where I live.
3. I am a real estate investor. I picked the top five performing *REITs (real estate investment trusts,* or large real estate investment companies that are publicly traded on the stock market) and bought shares through my brokerage account. This gives me geographic diversification because they are nationwide investments. Through this portfolio, I have residential, commercial, and industrial assets, and I have top industry professionals managing the properties. However, I also have full liquidity because I can sell my shares anytime.

Regardless of the returns each of these investors make on their investments, each example tells a different story, yet all three people identify themselves as real estate investors. Perhaps learning different abilities opens up more possibilities of investments, but the task here is to define a self-concept based on the current personal situation. The self-concept should evolve as the investor grows in knowledge and experience.

Skill learning

Skills are the basis of becoming a competent investor. The type of skills that an investor must learn will vary based on the type of investor they want to become. People will naturally be attracted to a type of investment based on their personal and professional backgrounds, as well as their natural abilities. But skill building requires using a personal background and combining it with training and practice to reach the goal of enhancing the required skills.

People typically progress within an area of skills when they put in the required effort and learn from experience. Depending on an individual's aptitudes, practice, and experience, a person can start off as a novice and incrementally improve their proficiency until they become an expert. As they become more advanced, the skills a person needs to develop will change. In part this is because skills start accumulating and integrating, which enables development of more complex skills.

For example, a child usually learns how to catch a ball with both hands but has trouble throwing it in a particular direction. In time and with practice, children can learn how to throw the ball better, using only one hand and in the desired direction. At the same time, they can learn how to catch the ball with the other hand. Developing both skills in both hands makes for more complex abilities and flexibility, which in time will increase the speed and accuracy of catching and throwing. It also improves hand-eye coordination and the sense of precision when it comes to catching the ball.

Just as catching and throwing skills can become more efficient and effective, investing can improve through skill-building. Newman and Newman, identified four principles to understand how complex behavioral skills are achieved.

1. The development of a skill depends on a combination of sensory, motor, perceptual, cognitive, linguistic, emotional, and social processes.
2. Skills are not always acquired as a sequence from simple to complex. In fact, they are developed as a simultaneous integration of many levels of components by working on simple and more complex aspects of the skill at the same time.
3. The natural limits of the person's system will constrain an individual's capacity to perform a skill. With practice, lower

levels' processes will become automatic so the person can focus on the higher levels of the process.

4. Effective skill application requires the use of strategies. People who become highly skillful operate with a goal in mind and observe their performance constantly. This way they can notice a discontinuity in performance, are selective on where they focus their attention, and can refine the higher order process as they perform the skill.[21]

To master the skill learning task of this stage, investors need to define what investment areas they want to focus on or what type of expertise they want to develop. While many aspects of investing are similar across investing strategies, there are specific aspects that need to be learned to improve proficiency in a particular investment type. A gold and silver investor needs a different set of skills and perhaps another perspective compared to a cryptocurrencies investor.

That does not mean a person cannot or should not diversify the type of investments they get involved with. In fact, a basic principle of investing is diversifying one's investments either to mitigate risks or to have multiple income streams. The number of investments, types of investments, and capital committed to someone's investment portfolio should increase gradually, however, and should go hand in hand with the development of the required skills to move into a new investment.

Maturation of decision-making biases

Decision-making is an entire field of study in itself. Economists want to understand how people make decisions because they like to measure and forecast everything. Marketers want to understand how people make decisions so they can sell more products or services. Psychologists want to understand how people

---

[21] B. Newman and P. Newman, *Development through Life.*

make decisions so they know more about human nature, and so on. The literature on financial and investment decision-making is so vast, a whole book could be written just to cite the references and resources.

The interest in decision-making for this book is from the perspective of maturing through the always-existing biases in making an investment decision. Literature has shown how people always have biases when making a decision. Biases come from gender, ethnicity, race, age, nationality, culture, religion, personal history, socioeconomic status, personal goals, level of education, emotions, and countless other factors.

Some biases could have a stronger influence. For example, Daniel Kahneman, author of *Thinking, Fast and Slow*, thinks that overconfidence is the most significant of the cognitive biases, particularly when making an investment decision.[22] Robert Shiller, an economics professor at Yale University and economics Nobel prize winner, thinks *irrational exuberance*, also known as animal spirits or a spontaneous urge to action, is one of the most important drivers of investment behaviors.[23] Both authors mentioned are Nobel prize laureates in economics, but just like them there are hundreds of highly qualified people trying to understand the whys and hows of investment decision-making.

From my perspective one thing is certain—it is possible to learn one's own biases. The higher degree of consciousness we have about our background, motivations, and goals for our investments, the easier it becomes to be aware of our personal biases. So exercising a higher degree of control over the biases becomes easier. Thinking about our own biases before making a new investment should always be a part of the investment strategy.

---

[22] Daniel Kahneman, *Thinking, Fast and Slow*.
[23] Robert J. Shiller, "How about a Stimulus for Financial Advice?," *New York Times*, 2009; Robert J. Shiller, *Irrational Exuberance*, 2000.

An example of a mature investor who is well aware of his biases and their need to be highly conscious of them comes from Warren Buffet. In a recent interview on CNBC, Buffet jokingly said, "I have someone in the office whose job is to keep me away from buying airlines." He mentioned that in his characteristic good sense of humor, but he was honest about his recurring impulse to buy airlines even after writing to his investors advising against such investments.

Through Berkshire Hathaway, Buffet has been one of the major holders of airline stocks including maintaining significant positions in the four largest US airlines. He initially had the thesis that people would keep increasing how much they fly and that airlines would at least hold their value. However, Buffet mentioned several times in his annual letters to investors how airlines were a terrible investment and even wrote that airlines were "a disaster for owners." He finally liquidated his positions in all airlines at a big loss in the pandemic of 2020.

It is possible to speculate and analyze why Buffet is so attracted to airlines. But Buffet's down-to-earth response is useful in showing us his awareness and proactive approach to managing such bias.

A sense of belonging to a peer group

Peer interaction is a common theme in psychosocial development throughout the lifespan. On a personal development level, peer interaction becomes more important in early adolescence when the peer group becomes more structured and organized than it previously was.[24] Roles grow into more defined functions, and the individual's participation in the group becomes more defined. Ideally it can lead to *a sense of belonging to a peer group of investors.*

Just like in adolescence, investors in the stage of unfolding acumen of inquiry have the task of expanding their horizons and

---

[24] B. Newman and P. Newman, *Development through Life.*

exploring the world of investments with less need to return to the safe base. Delving into the different options of investing strategies and meeting people who invest in different ways is a method to learn more about the investing world and the options available as well as a way to support the task of developing an investor self-concept.

Building a network that supports the investing endeavors is a must to become a successful investor. Even investors who go about their investing by themselves need to connect with people who can support or persuade against their decisions. This would be like an investor who decides to invest in stocks because they believe they can do everything by themself, creating and managing their portfolio from their computer or smartphone. They are much more likely to become successful if they would at least learn the basics of stock investing, gather pertinent information to support investment decisions, and continuously review and/or update their portfolio based on expert knowledge and peer recommendations.

To be successful, the investor should learn about investing in the stock market through any of the various options out there. They could take an in-person course at a serious institution, such as an intensive, weeklong course from a university's continuing education department, or a not-so-intensive course at universities' executive education department offered weekly or biweekly over several months. They can also take an online course created by true experts, people who would be hard to access in person because of different variables but who have created great online courses. Most major universities have developed beneficial content, which is also offered for free through their institution's portals. Just doing a search on the web or on social networks brings up many options for online education. And of course, there is always vast literature about stock trading, which is easily accessible through Amazon, Kindle, iBooks, and the like.

Then to continuously review and/or update their portfolio, the investor should constantly read analysts' opinions, at least review the news on pertinent stocks, and/or follow the experts on social media. Finally, the investor should also learn what other investors are doing (by joining an investors club), keep in touch with fellow course participants, attend conferences, and meet other investors with whom they should discuss present issues, needs, or aspirations.

To fulfill any or all of the undertakings mentioned, the investor will need to connect with other people who have similar interests. In this way, they would be getting involved with organizations or creating their own peer network that would build *a sense of belonging to a peer group*. There is a huge amount of power that derives from the feelings of belonging to a group, which will certainly boost the investor's feeling of certainty and security and will support their investment journey overall.

Investment Crisis: Drive vs. Inadequacy

The two leading forces creating the crisis for this stage are the opposing poles of drive and inadequacy. Momentum for growth and advancement through the stages comes from the successful resolution of the unfolding acumen of inquiry stage's crisis. The crisis in this stage is created because investors need to balance their individual drive and their feelings of inadequacy that can stall or even paralyze their growth as an investor.

In psychology, *drive theory* tries to understand psychological drives, which are instinctual needs that motivate the behavior of an individual.[25] The theory explains that organisms have natural psychological needs that create a negative state of tension when they are not met. Motivation creates an incentive to take action. When the needs are satisfied, the organism relaxes and returns to homeostasis.

---

[25] Sigmund Freud, "Three Essays on the Theory of Sexuality," in *The Standard Edition of the Complete Psychological Works of Sigmund Freud.*

In a stage of exploration, self-definition, skill building, and integration with peers, having the correct amount of motivation, drive, and initiative are key to pushing forward and navigating the challenges that occur. Cultivating a strong sense of autonomy, self-control, and confidence will support the development of motivation and skills to inquire and experiment.

People's motivations can also be framed by *classical economic theory*. The most basic form of this consumer choice theory states that people are motivated by the goal of achieving the highest level of satisfaction they can. They try to reach that satisfaction by buying as many goods and services as they can afford.

People do not necessarily spend all the income they receive in a particular period of time; they always have the choice of extending the time for using their income. In other words, there is always the option of saving and investing a part of the income. While investing a part of the income postpones the sought-out satisfaction that can be found through purchasing things, it also provides the promise of increasing the satisfaction at the achieved rate of return on the investments at a later time.

Consciously deferring a higher degree of satisfaction provides the opposite effect to an investor feeling inadequate. *Inadequacy*, the opposing side of the spectrum in this stage's crisis, has a wide range. The range spans from grounding an investor's impulses helping them to become more realistic, to bringing an investor to a standstill.

People often feel inadequate or inferior because of two things that can trigger such feelings—the self and the social environment. One theory that can help us understand a person's perceptions of their abilities is Alfred Adler's organ inferiority. Adler called *organ inferiority* a physical or mental limitation that prevents the acquisition of certain skills.[26] Anyone who cannot master certain skill feels inferior, to a certain extent.

---

[26] Alfred Adler, "The Fundamental Views of Individual Psychology," *Individual Psychology*.

Everyone knows that no one can do everything well because people cannot master every skill they try. Even people who are quite optimistic about tackling a new challenge will experience feelings of inferiority if they cannot really achieve the expected results. A process of comparison to others can potentially increase the feelings of inadequacy. Furthermore, the social environment can stimulate the inadequacy feelings by placing a negative value on failure.

The grim picture illustrated can bring an investor to develop feelings of helplessness. If someone falls into such a state, they would emphasize the negative aspects of the task attempted, disbelieve their successes, increase self-blaming, and would likely be looking for a way to escape the situation. Fortunately, things do not have to come to the worst-case scenario that was just described. The crisis can be resolved through the central process of education, which will be described next.

Central Process: Education

The concept of education is directly related to an individual's culture, and the term can have different meanings across the world's diverse cultures. For example, in English, education typically refers to formal or academic learning. The term *education* focuses on individual knowledge and skill development.[27] In Spanish, *educación* (education) has multiple meanings, depending on the context. The word on its own usually refers to proper and respectful social behavior, the type of learning that comes from home, parents, or family. However, it can also be used to describe formal academic instruction or even academic degrees. There are other cultures that even have words to separate meanings, as is the case in Hebrew. In Hebrew, there are two words that mean education: חינוך (phonetically: chinuch) a word that depending on the context can

---

[27] Patricia M. Greenfield et al., "Cultural Pathways through Universal Development," *Annual Review of Psychology.*

be used to describe formal education or parental education. But there is also השכלה (phonetically: hashkalah), which is only used for formal academic education.

Formal education has only been separated from hands-on learning at home with parents or the community for about 200 years. It was only after the industrial revolution that children started attending schools. Before that, children used to learn from their parents by helping with daily tasks at home. Children would participate in home chores, farming, commerce, and family and community traditions such as religious activities. This fulfilled education in its broadest sense. At its core, education means to pass on wisdom and skills across the generations. Most formal teaching now takes place in specially designated buildings, during particular hours, and with professionals dedicated to instructing, which has made schools primary authorities in education.

All this context is important because to this day, investors keep learning how to invest in formal and informal ways, and both can be effective. There is formally learning about economics, finance, investing, etc. in a business school or other educational institutions, as well as through formal training and experience by working for a business that enables this type of learning. Yet there is also hands-on education with family, perhaps just a mentor who is highly regarded given their abilities (but is not a professional teacher), or even people who are autodidacts and have the ability to learn on their own.

There are advantages and disadvantages to all approaches. For example, regarding the formal side, too much literature and academic theories without the practical experience can encapsulate an investor. It could close them into a frame that is not well adapted to current situations or that does not allow them to react quickly enough to some specific situation. On the other hand, learning from one person or just a few people could be a reductionistic view. And that could deter an investor from knowing all the options for investment strategies out there or from having a profound understanding of the context in which they are to invest.

Either through formal or familial education, the only way to resolve the conflict of drive versus inadequacy is by getting educated. Education will provide a frame and context to the internal disputes that can and will arise when considering an investment. The process of getting educated will naturally balance the impulses of too much drive or feelings of inadequacy.

If drive comes from the motivation to satisfy a psychological need, the best way to have a realistic need when it comes to investments is to set an attainable goal based on a plausible plan. To have a plan that can be effectively followed, the investment plan and goals need to be constructed through down-to-earth, accurate, pragmatic, and reasonable thinking—the kind of process that should come from an educated mind. Without the proper education, the investment plan is at risk of not being more than a fantasy, which could end up being very costly.

With proper education, feelings of inadequacy can also be subdued. Obtaining the proper skills required to participate in an investment will provide the investor a heightened sense of security for deciding about what they are getting involved in. Even if they were to compare themselves to other investors, they could see they have more or less skills or experience than others. But they wouldn't be at a complete loss when discussing an investment. They'd also have the resource of a proper network to consult about an investment in case they are still feeling inadequate about making a decision, which in itself reinforces the sense of security because they have a network backing them up.

How, where, and with whom an investor gets educated is relatively less important compared to the fact that education is absolutely necessary to become a mature investor. Once an investor has a better developed self-concept or an investment philosophy or thesis, it becomes much easier to find the proper education channels. Simply by being in the process of getting educated, the unfolding acumen of inquiry stage's crisis of drive versus inadequacy will become less intense, and the investor will be ready to successfully move on to the next stage.

Investor Adaptive Quality: Proficiency

With the correct education and experience, as well as successfully achieving the stage's tasks, an investor will acquire the adaptive quality of proficiency. *Proficiency* implies competence gained through training and experience. Erikson considered competence to be the "free exercise of dexterity and intelligence in the completion of tasks, unimpaired by infantile inferiority. It is the basis for cooperative participation in technologies, and it relies, in turn, on the logic of tools and skills."[28]

A proficient investor will achieve a sense of deep confidence in his abilities to engage in new situations and do well. Such sense will enhance the investor's self-esteem and enable them to walk into new situations with a more positive and optimistic expectation of doing well. While no investor thrives in 100% of their endeavors, a proficient investor might stumble upon an investment gone wrong, but they will experience it merely as a bump in the road.

Investors who achieve a sense of proficiency love to learn new things. They are people who love to keep on searching for investment opportunities and keep trying to move into different types of investments. They enjoy a challenge. In fact, new challenges are very exciting because the investor feels that they have what it takes to obtain the required skills for tackling the new undertaking. They also very much enjoy helping or teaching others, as it reinforces their sense of security about the skills they now have internalized. In contrast, an investor could be dispirited and lethargic. These are the people who develop the core issue of the stage, which is idleness.

---

[28] Erik H. Erikson, *The Life Cycle Completed: A Review*, 1982.

Core Issue: Idleness

When parents have continued guilt-inducing interactions with their children, the children tend to become inhibited. They don't become the children who keep trying to tackle a challenge and fail—they are children who are passive or withdrawn. Likewise, an investor who is unable to achieve the stage's tasks of acquiring the proper education or who fails to engage in the education process will not become proficient. They then run the risk of falling into idleness.

Idle investors who lack drive and stamina to move toward their investment goals don't know how to engage psychologically with the demands they encounter when getting involved with an investment. These are people who typically have trouble bringing about actions and have trouble changing the course of events. Therefore, they are people who are unlikely to solve problems by coming up with plans, analyzing them, and executing them. Investors in this situation will likely sit in idleness and will not be able to design an investment plan, let alone execute it.

Everybody experiences periods of not having enough energy or confidence to take action. Investors, just like anyone else, can become overwhelmed, have self-doubts, or question their own worthiness. People can survive for a while on autopilot, and investors can carry on doing what they know how to do routinely, especially if they don't really depend on their investments to live. However, eventually an investor's life will turn around and demand that they deal with new challenges and posit new expectations. When those times come, investors who fell into idleness will be unable to cope.

No one wants to fall into idleness, but it can happen to anyone. Investors should engage in the process of education to avoid becoming idle; education will also enable the investors to resolve the crisis of drive versus inadequacy and to continue growing. It's important to get educated, pay attention to the lessons learned from experience, and keep laser-sharp focus on the goals ahead to continue the forward momentum.

CASE STUDY 2
Dexterities in the Making

After buying the duplex where he now lived, Oliver felt he wanted more. More properties, more income, more self-sufficiency, and more freedom. Essentially Oliver had figured out how to get someone else to pay for him to live where he was now living. Not only that, but he owned the whole building. He was making money while he was sleeping—an investor's dream. Continuing with his day job only made sense because the remaining income from his single rent was not enough for him to live on, but he knew it was only a matter of time.

Oliver had now developed a strong interest in real estate investing. As much as he had dedicated to reading and learning about the topic, he knew he needed to complete more deals to enhance his experience as well as his income. He felt confident with researching, doing the due diligence, and even marketing and renting a property. One thing he needed more of at this point was money!

Oliver had already committed all his savings when he bought the property where he was living. He had little income from that, and he still had his job. Waiting for a while to gather funds before moving ahead with a subsequent investment was a sensible option. However, Oliver could not wait to continue the growth of his real estate empire. He decided to start looking around for other funding options. He figured that if he was going to wait until he had the same amount of cash he had for the previous deal he made, he would have to sit and wait for almost three years. That was not something Oliver could tolerate.

Oliver was keen on moving forward with his real estate investments. He had continued to read and learn ideas and strategies for investing in real estate. One strategy he heard about and wanted to explore further was buying an owner-financed property. That means he'd buy a property from someone willing to provide the financing of the purchase. Sellers do this by selling their properties in monthly payments instead of collecting the full values upfront. They also charge a percentage in interest, which means they sell at a higher final price.

If Oliver were able to find a property that the owner would sell to him in monthly payments, that would represent less than what he could rent the property for and he would be able to acquire a second property with little to no money upfront. He could also receive more cash each month again. Oliver jumped into a new search for a deal like that.

Searching for a property that fit all of Oliver's parameters was not an easy task. This time he was not going to be living there, so Oliver thought it would be easier to find a property that could be a good deal, but it proved to be a long and exhausting chore. Oliver was also working on this project in his spare time, while also trying to maintain free time to see his family, meet his friends, date, exercise, and practice his hobbies. This became a very intense period in Oliver's life, but he appreciated that he was also learning a lot about real estate investments.

Oliver started looking for his second property through the Realtor he had worked with before. But after a few unsuccessful months of searching, Oliver realized he would need to take different avenues to reach his goal. He contacted several Realtors who worked in his area, and he started asking friends and family if they or anyone they knew would be interested in his proposal. He even tried direct mailing to hundreds of houses in his area. It took him over six months, but Oliver finally found a prospect.

It was a Saturday morning when Oliver was walking down the street to his neighborhood coffee shop that he enjoyed. He'd gone at least a hundred times by a house that had a sale sign out, and he became curious about why that house was not selling. The house seemed to be in somewhat decent shape, and the neighborhood was up-and-coming. Oliver decided to call the listing agent to ask what the story was with the house.

Oliver went to visit the house with the listing agent. The house was somewhat dated but had good bones, and Oliver thought it would be somewhat of an easy fix. He was confident he could turn it around and make it nice again. He learned that the house was owned by a quiet, stubborn lady who would not sell for a penny under her asking price, which seemed a bit high but not an awful lot either.

Oliver kept inquiring and found out that the lady had moved in with her daughter when she listed the house for sale. The lady's husband had died recently, and the house was the only thing she had—she had no money nor income. She did not want to lower the price because she really needed the money to live, or at least, that was her story.

Oliver liked the location and the building, and he thought he could easily make the house look better and get it rented quickly. He ran the numbers on the property and figured it would make sense for him to buy it if the lady agreed to certain terms. The most important stipulation was that instead of receiving a large sum of money, the owner would be receiving a monthly check long term. The agent presented the offer to the owner, and much to Oliver's disillusionment she did not agree.

But Oliver was persistent. He was not going to let go so easily—he would not be defeated. A few days later, Oliver called the agent again and asked him to set up a meeting with the owner. The agent called back and said the lady was not interested in meeting. Oliver was a charming people person. He could read people and their reactions, knowing what to expect from them. He was hoping for the meeting, but in all honesty, he practically expected the lady to refuse so he had a plan B.

Oliver was determined to get that house, so he pursued his backup plan by writing a letter by hand, explaining a little about who he was and his intentions for the house, plus strongly stating that he was not a heartless businessman who just wanted to make money off her house. He was a young investor who lived in the neighborhood and really liked the house; he just wanted to bring it back to life and enable someone else to enjoy living where she once did. Oliver understood it was hard for her to let go of her home, and he could relate, as he had gone through significant losses in his own life. He also promised he would have the utmost respect for the house and would keep it intact, except for some aspects that could use some updating.

A few weeks later, the agent called Oliver and said the lady had read his letter and agreed to meet. She wanted to meet at the house in a couple days, and Oliver was overjoyed. He kept running through how he would present the whole idea of the owner-financing deal to the lady. In fact, he was so excited that he couldn't sleep the night before. Then the meeting day came. Oliver arrived early to the house and asked the agent to be there early too. He wanted to run the pitch by the agent to get feedback. The agent said it was a strong, compelling argument, and he did not see how the pitch wouldn't convince the owner.

The lady walked into the house with her daughter while Oliver was looking at his phone. When the agent introduced everyone, Oliver became speechless. He had been anxiously waiting and preparing for this moment, yet when they were there, Oliver could not articulate a single word. The agent called Oliver aside and asked if everything was all right with him and asked why he was not pitching his idea. Oliver said it was the daughter. The agent asked, "What is wrong with her?"

Oliver said, "Nothing. She is stunning! She is making me nervous, and my mind is blurred!"

The agent laughed, gave him a friendly nudge, and said, "Focus, man, focus."

Oliver settled down and was able to make sense with his arguments. He assured the lady he was a trustworthy person who would never miss a payment. He explained how she would be getting more money from selling her house this way than receiving the full sum upfront. All of the proper legal documentation for the deal would also be there to support and ensure everything ran smoothly. The owner seemed to be drawn to the offer, and her daughter seemed very interested in Oliver's presentation too.

A few days later, Oliver got a call from the agent to let him know they had a deal. Oliver was jumping for joy! It was an amazing way to get his second deal. He called his designer friend and did everything he did the last time to get the house ready. As soon as he closed on the house, Oliver worked nonstop to have the place ready to rent. Even though he had a tiny budget for renovations, Oliver got the house looking great and got it rented immediately. He now owned and managed two properties, both of which were providing some extra cash, and he managed to be cash flow positive again.

With a second stream of extra income, Oliver was one step closer to freedom. However, he was still quite a long way from living off of his investments' income. Nevertheless, this brought him new motivation to keep working his job, as he could almost taste how it was just a temporary situation. At this point, Oliver had a higher income, but he knew he needed to search for another deal similar to his last one.

Oliver knew finding owner-financed deals wasn't easy and that it would take time. But when the whole thing materialized, it would again only provide a small extra income. It would still take significant time for the three streams to amount to enough money to make another investment or a livable income, so Oliver was getting a little frustrated.

Oliver was starting to feel that real estate investments were something that took an endless amount of time to actually provide a sustenance. He really did not want to spend the next ten years working his job, so he thought perhaps he needed to experiment with something else. That reasoning brought back the idea of his friend who was building his stock portfolio.

The one thing Oliver knew regarding investing in stocks was that he could invest a really small amount of money. Oliver, being who he was, felt incredibly hesitant about the idea of investing in what he considered a high-risk investment. He also thought he could now afford to lose a few hundred dollars, even though he hated the idea. But of course, before investing a cent, Oliver read through a pile of books, took a few online courses, and opened a brokerage account just to follow the markets and familiarize himself with the system.

The day came when Oliver actually funded his account and decided to start trading. He now understood that when it came to the stock markets, there was trading and there was investing, but they were not the same thing. The former is speculative in nature and tries to make quick gains, while the latter has a long-term outlook. Oliver thought he was going to play around with a really small amount, which he considered doomed to be lost soon anyway. Much against his personality and nature, he decided to do some "risky" day trading, as he was trying to build up some gains he could add to his next real estate investment.

Oliver had selected a few publications and analysts he followed for investment recommendations, and he built his tiny portfolio based on their recommendations. He was lucky, and a week after his stock purchase, his tech stock soared by 34%. Oliver was in absolute awe; he knew to make a 34% return in a real estate investment would take years. He was starting to like this new game.

Oliver continued to add funds to his account to allow for more trading possibilities. He was really enjoying that he could have precise information on demand, anytime and anywhere, when it came to his portfolio performance. It wasn't so great on those days when the markets went down, though. When that happened, he couldn't stop checking the red numbers on his account every thirty minutes.

Oliver was learning a lot about finance, and after a while he could see how this type of investing was a long-term game. In the meantime, however, he had access to see where his finances were going, which in general were doing well. Yet Oliver was not really convinced about doing this type of trading long term. He spent most of the time being a nervous wreck and felt a need to check his portfolio and his email all the time. Plus there was no cash flow. After a while, he couldn't wait to have enough money to pull out so he could do another real estate deal. Then something happened, which gave him an idea....

One weekend Oliver walked to his usual coffee shop as he often did, except that day he ran into Natalie, the daughter of the lady who sold him the house nearby. Oliver was excited about coming across Natalie, and while he was still a bit jittery about talking to her, it was Natalie who approached him. She said she was glad he bought their house. Oliver was intrigued and asked why. Natalie explained that before he bought the house, a few people had been interested, but they all had the same thing in mind. They wanted to do a significant renovation and sell it, as the house was in an up-and-coming neighborhood. They all thought the people moving into the neighborhood wanted newer designs and construction, but her mother hated that idea.

Then Natalie asked him why he did not think about that, and voilà! Oliver thought to himself, *Why didn't I think of that?!* But he did not say a word about it. Instead, he said, "Well, I guess I have a different perspective on things, but I doubt you would be interested in listening to my story."

Natalie said, "I saw your presentation when you offered to buy the house. I was interested the first time." Oliver smiled, pulled up a couple of chairs, and they sat to have their coffee together. They ended up spending hours talking, foreshadowing for what was to come.

After Oliver descended from the clouds and got home that afternoon, he started working on the idea of flipping a property. He started thinking about how he could fund the project, searched for lenders, and even researched some crowdfunding websites. At the same time, he started searching for properties he could flip.

After some time exploring the market and seeing dozens of houses, Oliver found a little house not too far from where he lived that made the perfect candidate for his new project. Also, his broker was an experienced house flipper and had recommended Oliver to take that house. Oliver managed to secure funding with a 90% loan-to-value and a 100% of the renovations cost. He recruited his usual team: a home inspector, broker, and a designer. This time he was adding a contractor, and of course the lender. Oliver also hired a real estate attorney, which he'd learned about in his courses, to help him review all the legal documentation he'd be dealing with.

The project went mostly smoothly. The renovations were done in a few months, and the broker had a client ready to buy as soon as the house was done. Oliver had excelled in the crafting and execution of his plan, and he undertook what he had deemed a good option to raising his capital. And he succeeded. He had made a 14% return on the full investment, which meant he'd almost doubled his money. Oliver had invested only 10% of what the purchase value of the house was and after paying back the lenders, he had made an impressive return on the amount he had exposed to risk. And it was a bonus that the whole thing took less than a year to complete.

After that experience, Oliver thought he could wait and do a few more of these flips before going back to buying rental properties. He went through the same process once more, but this time he had more money, so he decided to buy a larger, two-unit building. Oliver was hoping to sell each unit separately and was working on the legal process for that. After a long battle with the local authorities, Oliver was not able to legally split them into two independent properties.

That was an unexpected blow. When the renovations were complete, the property had to go on the market as one entity, but the whole design had been made for the individualization of the units, so the place did not make much sense for most people.

Time was going by, and Oliver was unable to sell. Time was Oliver's worst enemy in this case because he was rapidly accruing debt through the loan's high interest rate. He had used the same hard money lender he used the last time, but the loans they provide had incredibly high rates. Oliver could not sleep, could not focus at work, was grumpy all the time, and felt at a loss for what to do with his newly renovated building. He even considered renting the unit where he lived and moving to the new building. But it was too far from his job, family, friends, and Natalie, and in a rougher neighborhood. Not a good option either.

Natalie and Oliver's relationship had become much closer by then and not seeing Oliver well, Natalie was concerned. One day she told Oliver that one of the interested parties who came to see her mother's house before had mentioned something about a real estate investors club, like an association or something like that. "Maybe you should join something like that," she said to Oliver. "You might find some guidance or ideas there."

Oliver remembered an organization he came across in one of the conferences he'd attended. It was a network of real estate investors, one that now might be a good time to join and ask for help.

Oliver joined the organization and posted his ailments with his latest project on the organization's forums. He soon received a significant number of ideas and stories from other people who were in the real estate investing business. These were people involved in every aspect of the business, and they were from all over the world. Among those, he received a message from an investor in his area, and he was asking to go see the property. Oliver joyfully went to his building with a savvy businesswoman who saw an opportunity in the property. She said it would be perfect for her rental portfolio if she could buy at the right price. In a desperate move, Oliver agreed to sell at a loss because he just wanted to be out of the problem. Oliver ended up losing about 20% of what he had invested, but he learned a few lessons and the monetary loss was not as bad as it could have been.

After the bitter experience, Oliver was not sure what he wanted to do next. He just didn't feel the same ambition and desire to keep growing his investments—he felt beaten, at a loss. The guilt was killing him. He was enjoying all the content and the interactions he was getting form the real estate investing organization he had joined, but his perspective had changed. It felt as if he were seeing all these ideas, questions, replies, and offers from a distance, as if he were no longer a participant in the game but just a mere spectator.

His work friend asked him frequently about his investment portfolio in the markets, but Oliver was not very enthusiastic about discussing it. Oliver had lost a significant part when he used it to be able to purchase his last building. All his gains had been wiped out and then some. But overall, he'd built a portfolio that was performing well, and while he was feeling down, his portfolio value was increasing rapidly. His exposure to the investor's organization was also providing more knowledge and time, allowing his savings to go up again. All of this was going on without him even being conscious about it.

The day came when Oliver was assigned a few tasks at his job he really was not interested in doing. He was strongly reminded why he set himself up to build an investment portfolio. Oliver gained newly found motivation to start thinking about growing his investments again. And it just happened that the organization he joined was having a conference in his area, which he gladly attended.

The conference was inspiring. Oliver had the chance to hear great stories of successes and failures from people he had developed substantial respect for, as he'd read their books and taken their lectures. He also met a lot of new people he greatly admired, and many were local to his area. His professional network and resources were growing. Oliver left the conference with a sense of strength and motivation to go out and look for a new project.

Soon thereafter, Oliver went on to find an interesting deal. With a heightened sense of security in his knowledge and experience, an improved team of professionals supporting and executing his decisions, and a place for him to bounce off ideas from other real estate investors, Oliver's project was a solid success. He managed to turn around a three-unit building that was now providing noteworthy cash flow.

As soon as that building was done and got rented, Oliver started searching for the next deal. It was not long before he found his next move. He brought in the same team and went over the same process. However, this time it was with a twelve-unit property, which made Oliver really feel like he was operating at a completely different level. He now owned and managed four properties comprising seventeen units, all of which were cash flow positive.

Oliver was really on his way to what he had wished for, but for now the management work was starting to be too much to handle in his spare time. He did not expect owning rental properties to be so demanding and time-consuming. Oliver's next move was to add a key component to his team: a professional management company to support his endeavors. After he handed all the heavy work to the managers, Oliver went back to being an investor. He was happy to pay for freeing up his time again, which allowed him to focus on what he really wanted to do.

The team Oliver had put together, the knowledge he had built, the experience he had collected, and the relationships he had built with other investors helped Oliver develop a sense of confidence in his decisions that strongly propelled him forward. Oliver consistently added to his real estate portfolio, focusing on residential units for young, lower-middle class because that is what he understood best. Over the next few years, Oliver added over a hundred units to his portfolio. Not every deal he made went great, and he made some mistakes again. But he had a much better sense of how to deal with those as well and a much stronger income base that held him through more steadily.

Also during this time, Oliver and Natalie's relationship had continued to grow. They actually had been living together in Oliver's apartment for a while but were thinking of moving to a larger place. Just before they started looking for homes, Oliver proposed to Natalie. They started looking for houses in more family-friendly neighborhoods, as they were starting to plan a life together. As much experience as Oliver had with properties and buildings by now, this house hunt turned out to be a vastly different experience.

Looking for a new home turned the process on its head for Oliver. All his negotiation and business skills had to be left aside for a while. He was in for a distinct type of negotiation, and a much more personal one at that. But then Oliver realized he and Natalie did unbelievably well with the whole thing, and he became aware of how much he had been learning about himself, his reactions, and how best to manage his urges and wishes. It was his own personal insights that allowed for him to behave this way in the house search, but he also realized that was what was enabling his investments to grow steadily.

Case Analysis of Stage 2: Unfolding Acumen of Inquiry

Here is the analysis on this part of Oliver's story in relation to the unfolding acumen of inquiry stage of an investor's development.

Developmental Tasks

1) **Developing the investor's self-concept.** In this stage, Oliver continued to develop his interest, as well as his skills, as a real estate investor. Being the conservative, high-need-for-control kind of person he was, Oliver felt investing in a solid asset he could manage was the right fit for him. He

experimented with different types of real estate investments, and he also tried other types of investments, such as the stock market. But he did not feel it was a good fit for his personality. Oliver was a highly determined person who liked thinking ahead, planning, and following through on his decisions and strategies. He was initially attracted to investing in real estate and decided to continue in that direction for many reasons, including his tenacity and need to hold on to his plans. The more he got into this type of investment, the more he was able to define his niche for investing. Oliver became clear about his risk tolerance, the type of product he looked for in the market, and the strategy he liked to follow for investing in real estate. The longer he did that, the more highly identified Oliver became with being a real estate investor.

2) **Skill learning.** While duration of this stage was not clearly stated in the story, it conveys the idea it went on for years for Oliver. Throughout this time, he was exposed to many opportunities, and sometimes was forced to develop his skills as an investor. He had several good and bad experiences. But as he became more and more focused on real estate investing, Oliver looked for more formal education that could continue enhancing his abilities. Of course nothing provides an opportunity to learn like getting hands-on experience. Oliver accrued vast experience throughout the stage of unfolding acumen of inquiry by getting more deals done than many people ever do in a lifetime. Oliver went from one deal in the previous stage to owning over a hundred units by the end of this stage. That growth allowed for him to build a team, refine his financial planning, create a system to find properties to buy, increase his knowledge about how to finance the purchases, enhance his ability to get his units rented with a positive cash flow,

and many other skills necessary for successful real estate investing.

3) **Maturation of decision-making biases.** At first, Oliver was too afraid of investing as his background and family history made him exceptionally skeptical of taking any risks with money. It took quite a while for him to get involved in his first investment, but then he became overly enthusiastic and had to deal with losses. He was also able to experiment with speculating with stocks. Again, he started at a very low level of commitment, but then he built up from there. He tried out a few strategies, which not only helped elucidate Oliver's self-concept as an investor but also provided experience in the area of decision-making. Oliver's main bias was not to take risks. Unconsciously he thought investing or taking any kind of risk with his assets meant losing everything he had. But through all the learning he did, he was able to continue with his investments and the more his investments grew, the more apt he was to make decisions.

4) **Sense of belonging to a peer group.** Oliver had been reading, taking courses, and trying to follow along with what he was learning. But it was not until this stage that he really started connecting with other real estate investors and professionals who could support his endeavors. Oliver went from a guy with an idea of buying some rental properties to becoming a real estate investor. In the process, he built a reliable team of professionals, he met other investors with similar interests, and he joined an organization that became a great resource. With all this supportive network, Oliver achieved extraordinary growth in his property portfolio. He had grown into his new role. Connecting deeply to his role as a real estate investor, Oliver eased into relating to other real estate investors as equals.

Investment Crisis: Drive vs. Inadequacy

The opposing forces that create the unfolding acumen of inquiry's crisis can be seen operating throughout the stage. Oliver experienced periods of higher drive and periods where he felt inadequate. However, there are a few instances in which one of the poles becomes much more salient and shoved Oliver into crisis mode. As long as Oliver was able to find a way to go back and find momentum again, he was able to keep seeking balance, and the opposing forces become a catalyst for him to forge ahead. Oliver had to be in crisis to find the best way to resolve the crisis. Some of the times Oliver was in crisis mode are the following.

After his first investment, Oliver became enamored with buying rental properties and could not wait to get more. His drive was huge at that point. He managed to make a second deal, which turned out not to be an easy feat. But he successfully closed the deal, which inflated his sense of self further. The overexcitement built such a degree of drive that he overextended his abilities taking a risk with a deal he could not really back. So he encountered problems.

Oliver was hit hard with the issues he ran into with the third building he bought. He wanted to make a quick and highly profitable turnaround that proved to be more difficult and riskier than he'd anticipated. He ended up dealing with significant stress for a long time and feeling down even after he was able to be out of the problems. After that, Oliver moved strongly into the inadequacy pole and had no energy to get back into the investing scene for a while.

Oliver had enough social support that he was able to climb out of his misery and start to think that he still had options. He'd luckily attended an inspiring event that helped him get back on his feet. The event and the organization Oliver joined became incredible aids in improving his knowledge and even provided the opportunity to build a stronger team. Oliver got past his pain and moved into a strong period of growth and success.

The above examples demonstrate how Oliver went from inadequacy pole to the drive pole, to finding a better balance in between. He obtained enough drive to keep growing but became alert of not taking too much risk and of not going out of his emerging area of expertise. Oliver also learned not every deal he made would be great, but he accumulated much better resources to deal with the issues that could arise, and his expectancies became more realistic.

Central Process: Education

This long stage brought upon the conflict of drive versus inadequacy as was described before. But what helped Oliver build momentum and a resolution to the conflict was the central process of education. The better prepared Oliver felt to deal with the issues that catapulted him to a far end of the drive-inadequacy spectrum, the easier it was for him to find a balance and keep moving forward.

Because of his personality, Oliver had been very concerned with acquiring knowledge. Oliver had been reading and learning about real estate investments since the previous stage, but it was in this stage that he really started to get significant hands-on experience. He not only continued learning from different sources to make real estate investments but also started learning and getting involved in different types of investments.

Trying out different investment strategies is a normal part of the process for this stage. In Oliver's case, he was more conservative and felt better to not go out and experiment too much with his assets. He still tried out a few different ideas, and it was by educating himself that he is able to move forward with his urge to explore other options.

After he felt lost in an ocean of problems with the property where he did not do well, Oliver had a personal crisis. Yet the value of education became palpable after he sought further education to resolve his crises. Education in this case came in the form of meeting other, more experienced real estate investors. Oliver also expanded his education by attending a conference and from building a solid team of professionals with more knowledge and experience in complementary topic and skill areas. Through more and more deals, he kept building on his hands-on experience, which is the best form of education he could have received.

Investor Adaptive Quality: Proficiency

Oliver went through a lengthy process that took him through ups and downs, exciting achievements, and hard-to-take setbacks. However, while Oliver was slowed down at some points, he learned his lessons and was able to keep going. The more education and experience he got, the more confidence he gained to continue his forward momentum.

Oliver achieved the investor adaptive quality of proficiency after he became a clear, consistent, and successful real estate investor. When he was better able to resolve the conflict of drive versus inadequacy, Oliver clearly had a positive resolution, as he came out of the conflict to continue building a strong real estate portfolio. Oliver experienced how not everything will always be smooth sailing, but he became much more relaxed about continuing with his endeavors. Even if it meant running into issues, Oliver was not as apprehensive anymore because by getting through this stage, he developed a profound sense of competence in his area of interest.

CHAPTER 5
Stage 3: Sophisticated Skills, Sound Identity

Developmental Tasks:

1. Work discipline and management of life's demands

2. Lifestyle and investment plans

3. Investment philosophy

Investment Crisis: Expanding vs. Aridness

Central Process: Inventiveness

Investor Adaptive Quality: Commitment

Core Issue: Neglect

Having achieved proficiency as an investor, the individual who is now well into their investment quest is on to the next stage where they will also spend a significant stretch of time, as long as they are consistent with the undertaking. The investor who made it to this stage by successfully completing all the previous tasks is now someone developing sophisticated skills and a sound identity as an investor. The *sophisticated skills, sound identity* stage is a time to solidify their abilities and capitalize on the hard work accomplished thus far.

When things are going well, this should be a time for expansion both in areas that have yielded results as well as other new areas. If stretching into new areas of investing, the investor will be required to go back into skill development for such new endeavors. That said, skill building is much easier now because the investor has a solid base to build on. Increasing knowledge is merely adding on to the already established skills, which in turn are the stalwarts leading the acquisition of a new skills or knowledge. The same is true for incremental expansion of the network of contacts that can support the investing journey. As that network grows, so do the new investment opportunities.

Sophisticated skills, sound identity is also a time to test whether the investor's skills, decision-making abilities, and overall investing maturity have actually been moving in the right direction. Any investor's initial motivation to start an investing journey is to increase their financial wealth, income, or revenue streams. By now the investor must have gotten involved in more than one investment strategy and should be realizing gains. The investor undoubtedly is accruing not only personal achievements but also financial profits. If this is not true, then it's a sign that the investor needs to go back and review what needs to be changed or learned and matured. If they were to continue down the same path, they would run into a stagnation in their earnings or even worse.

Whether there is expansion or stagnation is what will generate the investment crisis of the stage. Diversifying (expanding) the number of investments, investment strategies, network of contacts, and income is on one end of the spectrum. The other end is aridness, which for this book means "to be dry and unproductive." Let's say the investor tried out a few strategies that they somewhat understood and thought would work, but in reality, it has led to decreased growth and a desiccation of new ideas.

To find balance between the poles of the investment crisis, *inventiveness* is the central process that needs to occur. Being inventive means that investing and any strategy or endeavor undertaken is only limited by the investor's creativity. Any issue that comes along, any discontinued project, or any heavy situation can always be figured out and disentangled to decide the best way forward use of a creative solution. The challenge is to become proactive and ponder the available options, many of which may not present themselves so easily. Yet a resourceful, inventive investor should be able to create solution options, so his investment plan can keep moving forward.

When an investor is unable to achieve the stage's tasks and become inventive, they can fall into the core issue of neglect. Disregarding issues with their investments, failing to problem-solve or simply faltering to expand are all actions that contribute to an investment plan collapse.

On the other hand, if the sophisticated skills, sound identity's tasks are mastered, the investor will move on to obtain the investor adaptive quality of commitment. A committed investor is able to stay on course with his investment plan and sort through all the difficulties any investment journey will bring about. They are committed not only to make their plan work but also to their personal growth, financial growth, and improvements for the greater good.

Developmental Tasks

Work discipline and management of life's demands

Work overall is a major topic for any adult. Balancing work and family life is one of the main issues in adult life, and adding the investment component only makes it more complex. Almost every adult has to juggle a number of commitments to a significant other, children, parents, and friends. Not to mention they also want to exercise, do recreational things, or practice hobbies. And if that weren't enough, there are always social commitments one must attend.

Trying to keep up with all of life's demands can certainly be overwhelming. Adding the component of being an investor will not reduce any of the tension. If someone misses a family gathering, they might get frowned upon the next time they meet, but if they miss paying taxes, the government might be a bit more aggressive in their response. An overload in life's demands can be a heavy burden, which can significantly impact life satisfaction. Even worse, this can contribute to dissatisfaction in life and generate a decline in a person's mental health and sense of well-being.

When someone decides to become an investor, the time dedicated to their investments has to be treated as serious work. Whichever way the investor decides to strategize and get involved in their investments, they need to factor in the attention the investments will require.

Work comprises a significant part of the activities an adult engages in, especially in terms of everyday occupations and energy put into social relationships. It also creates a large part of the frustrations and satisfaction in adult life. When an individual is also an investor, all of this gets multiplied and the emotional balancing becomes more complicated as well as absolutely necessary.

Investors' work can be organized in a variety of ways. The first requirement to become an investor is to have initial capital to invest, which in most cases comes from earnings and savings sourced from a day job. In those cases, the investor needs to keep working their job because it is the main income that provides not only capital for investing but also life support.

A long-term plan for people in such cases is important when it comes to determining their investment interests. Some of the questions they should ask themselves are:
- *How active an investor can I be?*
- *How much time do I really have to dedicate to my investments?*
- *What do I want to achieve with the investments made?*
- *Is this investment supplemental income? Of long-term value? For early retirement?*

The answers to these questions can help an investor define which investments are suitable.

While at the stage of sophisticated skills, sound identity, investors have already developed skills and should be involved in more than one investment. But this is also a time to reflect on what has been learned so far and foresee how to capitalize on that moving forward. Then based on their plan, an investor must develop and maintain the discipline to stay on track and following through with their investments. The main challenge for this case is having or making enough time to be able to effectively manage their investments.

Not every investor falls into the category of having to keep a job while also wanting to become an investor. Some people have a situation in which they don't need a day job to sponsor their investor endeavors. People who could be in this situation include but aren't limited to partners of people with successful corporate careers or successful professionals, people who are retired, or people who (for different reasons) received a sum large enough that provides a livable income from profits generated through good investments. There are also cases of people who suddenly receive large sums of money from severance packages, selling businesses, receiving inheritances, or perhaps even winning the lottery. And some people successfully build up their investments to the point of not having to keep a job anymore.

All the previously mentioned cases are people who can become full-time investors. It might seem counterintuitive, but in all of these cases, people will need to be much more disciplined about structuring their investing work. Being a full-time investor can be very demanding. Of course the time demand, just like all the other variables around investing, will depend on the type(s) of investments the investor decides to get involved with. Becoming a full-time investor is a personal decision as well as a matter of planning and financial possibilities. Among the many advantages of becoming a full-time investor, the main one is that you work for yourself and time management is your own responsibility.

Investing can also be done by managing a portfolio that only needs attention twice a week for an hour. The important part in this case is consistency. In the case of light management portfolio, the investor will also need to go through all the stages of development to become a mature investor, but perhaps using more time for managing their investments is not part of their life plan. An investor can still be successful operating this way, but the discipline of keeping strict supervision over their investments is still necessary for success.

Whether the investor is a passive investor who invests in a couple of *ETFs* (*exchange traded fund*s, or a type of security that includes a collection of securities, such as stocks) or a private fund, or a full-time, highly engaged and diversified investor, having work discipline is imperative. Therefore, developing effective work habits is important in this stage of sophisticated skills, sound identity. How much time, how to structure the work, and what the work in itself entails is what needs to be sorted through. Yet all of that will be determined in part by the general investment plan.

Lifestyle and investment plans

Lifestyle refers to all of the things people usually do regularly or fairly consistently in life; it's the way a person lives their life. It is a psychological construct that integrates the pace of activities, work, leisure, social relationships, and events. One's lifestyle guides decisions about how to organize time and prioritize the use of resources.[29] A *lifestyle* is based on values, interests, choices, and commitments, and their integration is perceived in how a person

---

[29] Basil G. Englis and Michael R. Solomon, "Where Perception Meets Reality: The Social Construction of Lifestyles," *Values, Lifestyles, and Psychographics*.

brings all of these into action, and in how much time and energy they dedicate to each area of their life.

Lifestyle is an important concept because every person who decides to become an investor begins their journey because they want one thing: to grow their wealth. The reason they want to grow their wealth is to sustain their lifestyle after they retire from their main job. Or perhaps some people want to change their lifestyle and have access to things they currently do not. Some people even have clear goals for why they want to increase their income, such as wanting to buy a house, wanting to travel more, or the ability to pay for their children's college education. But whatever an investor's reason is for increasing their wealth, it is directly related to their lifestyle.

Having a heightened maturity in defining the lifestyle an investor wants can help in the development of an investment plan. This awareness can provide a clear picture of the goals and the possibilities to actually reach such goals. A more seasoned investor knows what they are really capable of making with their investments and can outlay a plan based on their resources available and their lifestyle goals.

Not having maturity in outlining a lifestyle usually creates problems very quickly. The problems take different forms depending on the individual values, but it typically means over-stretching their possibilities and overcommitting to expenses they cannot really afford. A part of being an investor is understanding that history can provide information, but the past does not determine the future.

Falling into the type of issues described above can be extremely stressful for anyone. Unfortunately, some people think they can solve the issues by neglecting them. That attitude only intensifies the problems and also creates the stereotype that investors are self-absorbed sociopaths. The real issue is a lack of development as an investor, but sadly in some cases, that does get combined with a lack of ethics. In a few more extreme cases, someone with a significant psychopathology and a lack of ethics can cause severe issues to others.

Investment philosophy

While it's ideal to have an investment philosophy before a person starts making investments, it rarely ever happens. The same is true for most companies, and their philosophy is one of the basic aspects that must be developed. But most companies work on their philosophy after they are already operating, and investors can do the same.

When someone starts making investments, they are mostly concerned with the investment as well as their ultimate investment goal. The goals can be a change in lifestyle or funding children's college costs. But by the sophisticated skills, sound identity stage, the investor has been exposed enough to investments and has had enough experience with success and disappointments. And they've developed a solid identity as an investor. Therefore, investors should learn not only how to focus on their areas of expertise but also on having clear investment philosophies.

An *investment philosophy* is a set of core values and beliefs that guides investing. The philosophy is a way of thinking that can always be used as reference to create new strategies. A strategy is a way of bringing the philosophy into action. To develop an investment philosophy, an investor must have had enough education that they can sort through the many options out there, as well as integrate them with personal perspectives.

As an example, some of the better-known investment philosophies, which are usually associated with public markets investors, are value investing, growth investing, and socially responsible investing. *Value investing* is where an investor seeks companies that they believe to be currently underpriced and whose values will eventually rise significantly. *Growth investing* occurs when investors buy into companies whose services or products they believe will generate strong earnings in the future. *Socially responsible investing* is when investors select companies to invest based on the companies' impact on society and the environment.

To figure out which of these options resonate with someone, investors also need to think about their beliefs of things such as market efficiency, market behaviors, and overall human nature. There's also a myriad of variables to consider when developing a philosophy such as risk aversion, time horizon, tax status, and need for cash.

All of these variables make developing an investing philosophy complicated, which is exactly why some time should be dedicated to have a clear and well-defined philosophy. Also, by engaging in the process of considering all the nuances of the investment process, the investor is growing personally and achieving a higher degree of maturity.

Having an investment philosophy supports having a sound identity as an investor, which is why this task is part of this stage. It may seem that this task should have been tackled before, but it is difficult to have a clear investment philosophy without having enough experience. Investors also usually follow their personal core values in an intuitive manner when making their first investments.

Novice investors are usually unable to name or explicitly express their philosophies, but they have a general sense of what they are looking for and how they want to take on their initial investments. Achieving an elevated level of maturity means having the language to describe what they do, having clear guidelines they follow, and having had the experience of actually engaging in their chosen philosophies and strategies more than once.

Investment Crisis: Expanding vs. Aridness

The sophisticated skills, sound identity's crisis comes from the investor's pressure to be committed and improve their investing skills and from scrutinizing investment results. In order for their abilities, investments, and overall wealth to expand, the investor needs to be proactive, productive, and creative.

To *generate*, or to bring into existence, is one privilege of being an investor. Some investors focus on impact investing because they not only want to make a profit out of an investment, but also they want to make an impact in the world. Supporting or developing ideas that will introduce new things to the world, increase the production of things, or bring needed services to more people are ways to escalate an investor's productivity and provide different options in which an investor can expand.

This is also a point in which investors should start to feel an obligation to contribute to society. The perspective on the impact of their investments should also expand and strive to improve the quality of life not just for themselves but for future generations too. As people recognize the inevitability of mortality, they're often inspired to think more about future generations' well-being.

The most important and usually overlooked factor in any investment is time. While time is infinite, our time on this planet is not. The same is true for our time as investors. There is a limited amount of time for running investments, which depending on when a person became an investor, can be longer or shorter. But time should always be factored into one's investment plan.

It is also important to consider time when trying to measure the degree of spreading out. It's difficult to measure and put into numbers, but spreading out involves certain concepts that can be evaluated to provide a sense of where one stands. A part, and perhaps a significant one, comes from financials and the economic growth that an investor has achieved. However, there are other aspects of the expansion that are also important, such as a sense of growth of self, a realization of goals, a sense that one is making a difference in the lives of others, and/or even an active involvement in the growth of others.

In general, the theme of expanding versus aridness prevails through the psychological dynamics of the active life of an investor. *Aridness* means there is a lack of psychological movement or growth, and it happens to those who become unable to deal with all the challenges the investing life brings upon. Needless to mention, when there is no psychological movement, there will also be financial stagnation.

People with higher levels of neuroticism are at higher risk of falling into aridness. Neuroticism is associated with high levels of worry and a need for control. When these traits become triggered, these individuals can go into a freeze mode that will not let them keep moving.

Aridness is different from depression. Depressed people think of themselves as worthless, and they do not perceive themselves as people with resources to provide to their society. They usually have low self-esteem, question opportunities for future improvement, and therefore simply have no interest in investing. They lack energy and do not care to think of future possibilities.

In contrast, aridness can happen because an investor becomes comfortable with the headways they have been able to achieve, and the growth rate slows down. That decreased growth rate could come to a stop and even to a drawback if the investor is not careful. Investors need to realize that if they do not take new risks, their quality of life will deteriorate.

Investors who realize they are falling into aridness risk the possibilities of feeling outdated by new investment strategies and/or technologies, overstrained by role demands and maybe even isolated and without support. These periods of crisis can make an individual want to withdraw from their social networks as a process of self-protection, which can result in permanent lack of movement and progress. However, such periods may also bring about new resources that enable a person to see things from a different perspective, helping them get moving again into growth and expansion.

Central Process: Inventiveness

To help resolve the investment crisis of the sophisticated skills, sound identity stage, a balance must be sought. The process to find solutions is fueled by being inventive. *Inventiveness* means to have the power or ability to create new or original ideas, which redefines a world perspective and opens up new possibilities.

Finding themselves in a multiplexity of roles and life demands, investors need creativity to manage all of what is required of them. The same is true about managing the range of investments they now have and the problems they face. The difference between an investor who is thriving and spreading out with one who has become stagnant and arid is the capacity for inventive responses to the problems encountered in their investing journey. Every single investment will bring along a series of issues—the more creative the investor is, the easier it will be for the investor to solve them. Nevertheless, the high demands of life for an investor at this stage are stimuli enough to bring about creative problem-solving.

Inventiveness is rooted in childhood. When kids, usually toddlers, play with the "as if" way of thinking, they are learning how to imagine situations from different angles. Children learn how to use known objects for something entirely different as what they usually use them for, they give new names to familiar things, they imagine roles in their games, and all of these imaginary creations constantly change.

All these capacities for symbolic play are the foundations of creativity, which will be used later on in life in different ways. Everyone is creative in the sense that every human needs to cope at some point with life changes and unpredictable environments. In the case of an investor, it can be the development of their investment strategy or readaptation of a plan in response to a new situation. Perhaps the investor needs to decide on the best tax strategy or how to best weather a difficult economic outlook.

All of these examples call for inventiveness because each individual is unique, just as their investment situations are. The creative process always involves taking risks and running into frustration. That is the nature of the process because when inventiveness needs to be engaged, it is because the standard way to get through an issue is not working, which means there is no effective, predetermined method that can be applied to the situation.

Failure is always a possibility when devising new, uncharted approaches. And for some people this can create a lot of anxiety. However, through risk-taking, even when there are occasional failures but a predominance of successful efforts, people develop a sense of finding what gives meaning to life.

Investor Adaptive Quality: Commitment

Commitment is the quality that is associated with successfully achieving the tasks for this stage. To be *committed* means to care for the ideas and plans one has learned to develop. It also means to be concerned with the people such investments will benefit. The beneficiaries could range from generating employment to supporting the economy to the ultimate goal of increasing the investor's wealth and/or income to further support or change their lifestyle and that of their families.

Coming up with an investment philosophy, creating investment plans, and rendering an effective work discipline are no easy feats. All these achievements require effective and efficient follow-through to bring about the desired yields. When the returns are in fact being produced, that means the investor has developed enough commitment to see their growth prosper.

Commitment needs to be proactive. Investors have to work on caring for what they are developing and continue to be consistent with their beliefs and plans. That does not mean that a different direction cannot be taken when something is not working as expected, but it does require commitment to the ultimate goal in order to be adaptive to changing conditions. As the crisis of expanding versus aridness is resolved in a positive direction, investors find new energy and fresh forms to express their capacity for commitment.

Core Issue: Neglect

Neglect refers to two issues that can arise at this stage: lack of follow-through and ignoring the issues at hand. First, neglecting to follow through on the ideas and plans an investor has conceived. Abandoning or losing patience is a guaranteed way to under-perform on an investment and could create a risk of losing on the assets invested. Second, investors can neglect to realize something is not going well and that there are other ways to resolve an unfortunate situation rather than rigidly adhering to the original plan. It is one thing to be committed to an idea, but not accepting one's mistakes can be very costly.

When someone is highly committed to a certain idea, it's possible they might reject any idea that seems to differ because dissimilar perspectives and propositions could be perceived as threats. Erikson referred to such process of rejecting ideas as *pseudospeciation*; in his explanation, he referred to a person defining another group of people as different, hence dangerous and even potentially less human than one's own.[30] It is pseudospeciation that can create scapegoats out of family members, and it can build rivalries between communities. On a larger scale, this can create racial or religious feuds that can, and historically have, evolved into terrible destruction and even brought countries to war.

When an investment is not going as expected, it runs the risk of becoming neglected. Through pseudospeciation, an investor can start discriminating against lower-performing investments, psychologically building up hatred against the disappointing results the investor is obtaining. If a project falls out of the circle of commitment, it presents the risk of building stagnation to the investment portfolio. Not just because of mathematically bringing down the average returns, but because of the psychological effect of not caring for a plan devised.

Having faced a new crisis in the stage of sophisticated skills, sound identity, the investor went through the central process of inventiveness. There are many factors that will determine the degree of how creative an investor can become when facing a challenge, but everyone is capable of being inventive. Hopefully the investor resolves the crisis positively and will not develop a habit of neglect that can keep them from moving on to the next stage.

---

[30] Erikson, *The Life Cycle Completed*, 1982.

CASE STUDY 3

Prosperous Proliferation

After a beautiful wedding, Oliver and Natalie had been living in the house they bought for some time and were expecting their first baby. Oliver had reached the tipping point that allowed him to become a full-time investor—he no longer needed to work his day job. It had been very important for him to keep his job to make sure he would be earning enough and because it had allowed for his investments to grow at a much more rapid pace. If he had been using the income he was receiving from his investments for sustenance, it would have taken him a lot longer to build what he had been able to put together.

Oliver was now also thinking to scale up his investment portfolio by adding larger multifamily properties. He figured the due diligence and overall work required to make an investment in a larger residential property would be almost the same as what he had been doing so far, except the numbers would be larger. If things worked out well, he would be earning a lot more and a lot faster. Besides, he'd been successful with a twelve-unit building before, so it was just a matter of finding the right building.

Oliver started looking for the right building to buy, but it turned out to be more difficult than he expected. Competition in this sector was tough, especially in his area. Oliver had built a reputation with creditors, contractors, managers, and Realtors. At this point, finding the money to support his ventures was not very hard. Renovating and renting his properties was not that big of a challenge either. However, he was learning now that finding a great deal was a lot tougher than having the money and/or everything else needed to turn around these properties and make a profitable investment.

Oliver being as highly determined and focused as he was started dedicating almost all his time to the search for the right building to buy. After a while he decided to expand his horizons and start looking in other areas and not just where he lived. Even though he wasn't as familiar, properties in different states seem to offer better returns, not to mention the possibilities for finding a great deal were better when he had more options to consider. He resorted to his network and started traveling and looking at a few options he considered worthwhile.

After some time, Oliver decided to engage in a project where he bought a sixty-unit building pretty far from where he lived. It was not easy for someone with a high need for control, such as Oliver, to commit to investing in a physical asset that was so far away. He also had to build a new team from scratch. All these factors made the project highly stressful, on top of traveling back and forth often. The travel was time-consuming and tiring, adding to the investment costs.

Time went by, and things worked out with the latest building. Oliver found a good management company through people he had met in the real estate investors organization he'd joined. The building's rehab took longer than expected and not everything was to Oliver's complete liking, but the investment was cash flowing, which made Oliver happy. Natalie, however, was not thrilled with Oliver being so consumed by work, which now included significant travel. On top of it all, they now had a baby who would not even let them sleep! Life was getting more complex.

Natalie was starting to question Oliver: "You left your job to be an investor, and now you are working more than ever before. You keep traveling, which keeps you away for days at a time constantly. And when you are here, you spend more than ten hours a day in your office." Oliver was conflicted—he saw Natalie's point, but he'd also successfully increased his portfolio by over 30% with just one deal. That deal was too good, and not continuing on that route would avoid a path to much faster growth. Oliver also agreed that this last building made him travel a lot at first. But once the building's renovations were done and it was rented, stabilized, under the management team, and receiving cash flow, he wouldn't be traveling anymore.

Oliver waited just a few months before he started looking for another building in the same area as the last one. He started traveling which again brought stress to the family's dynamics. As great as the investments Oliver was finding were, he knew this wasn't going to work long term. It was too much stress and too much work—this was not his idea of what an investor should be doing. He'd left his job and traded it for another, more demanding one.

For this project, Oliver's mother and brother asked to invest some money with him. Oliver agreed to partner with his family and manage the investment for everyone. With all the funds combined, he managed to purchase a hundred-unit building. He now had a local team he already knew, so things worked out more efficiently this time, and the travel decreased. Oliver was less preoccupied with being present to witness every step of progression for the building and the project overall.

In his travels for the second building, Oliver spent a lot of time thinking about how to better structure his time. Oliver also had a growing family and his mother and brother, who he enjoyed seeing. But he did not see his friends often anymore. He was also an avid tennis player and runner, but he had not been able to play or run much. So his goal was to be able to only work four to six hours, five days a week.

Oliver had all his investments to look out for, and he wanted to continue expanding. He'd been strongly increasing his real estate portfolio, but he'd also been allocating part of his income to his stock portfolio. He was not doing any heavy trading but had decided to keep searching for great companies he thought would be good long-term investments. He wanted to buy and hold for the long term.

Oliver realized he was at a point where he needed to do some serious thinking. He wanted to be able to have more social, family, and leisure time and a lighter workload. He was settled with being a real estate investor, but he wanted to find a way to make it less time-consuming. With so many other important things going on, Oliver realized those would only become more and more demanding as well. He was afraid that if he didn't prioritize the continuous growth of his investments, his income would stall, expenses would grow, and everything was going to collapse.

It was also a time for Oliver to think again about the purpose of his investments and overall strategy. He now had a comfortable life, but he could foresee how the costs of life would keep on increasing, just as much as his responsibilities and personal demands. Oliver knew the importance of continuing to grow his income, but he didn't want his workload to grow too. He had a decent stock portfolio that was a very passive investment and was growing in value, which he considered his retirement fund. He really liked how little he had to dedicate to building that investment. Unfortunately, real estate investments were not as passive as he would have liked. (At least they had not been so far.)

Oliver had become a wine connoisseur and a member of a club of wine enthusiasts who met once a month for a dinner lesson. Around that time, a new member had joined, and Oliver happened to sit next to him at the monthly gathering. When they were talking, the typical question of "What do you do?" came up, and Oliver said he was a real estate investor. The new member said, "Well, I happen to have some real estate investments as well, but that's not really something that keeps me busy."

Oliver replied, "The thing is, that's what I do full time. I do work with property managers, but I still have to review all the mail I get from my properties, make payments, do taxes, bookkeep, and so on. It all takes an awful lot of time, not to mention strategizing and the continuous search for new investments."

The man replied, "Wow, that sounds like a full-time job, which is why I decided to invest in a private fund that takes care of almost all those things for me."

As he returned home, Oliver kept playing with the idea of transitioning to investing in a fund, where things would be much more passive. He'd heard about that concept before in the real estate organization, but he always thought it was somewhat of a sophisticated property management that kept all the control of the properties. As an investor he also would not have a say in what went on and would not have any kind of liquidity either. Besides, he had developed the type of expertise those kind of investment funds charge for, so he didn't feel he needed to pay for that knowledge.

As time went by, Oliver kept playing around with the idea of the funds in his mind and came to a few conclusions:

1. By investing through such vehicles, he could further diversify his investments into areas where he did not have that much expertise.
2. He would be paying for work he knew how to do, but he would also be paying to free up his time and clear his mind of burdens and responsibilities.
3. His knowledge and experience in the field would be his strongest assets in evaluating and selecting with whom to invest.
4. He could even search for a company that would appreciate his expertise and allow him to be more participative than the average passive investor.
5. He could gain access to geographical diversification without having to engage in unlimited research and countless hours of traveling, not to mention the added costs.

All of these points made a strong case for Oliver to start searching for a private fund he would feel comfortable investing in. The first resource he used was again the organization he already knew, and it just happened that the annual conference was coming up soon. Oliver traveled to the conference and spent his time there asking around and talking to people who managed private funds. At the end, he went back home with a list of seven potential firms he was interested in, and he was even more excited because he found things he had not even considered, such as the possibility of doing international investments.

Oliver spent some time researching and talking to the people on his list. His due diligence was now concentrated on analyzing how other people were going about making real estate investments. Fortunately, he had plenty of knowledge and experience to rely on. He came down to three options that seemed like good choices, but he decided to work with two of them.

Oliver chose those companies for different reasons. One was a local company Oliver knew by name; he'd talked to them extensively, and they agreed to let Oliver have a seat on the board. Oliver was incredibly happy about that situation. He could continue using his expertise by participating in important, large-scale decisions, but he would not have to do all the work that was mechanical and time-consuming. Even better was that they had agreed to buy a significant part of Oliver's portfolio.

The second company he liked was focused on overseas investments. They'd recently been growing their acquisitions in Latin American tourist hubs, where the returns on the investments were particularly high. Oliver loved the Mayan Riviera, where they were currently focused, and the idea of owning a piece of paradise was especially enticing to Oliver.

Oliver now had to go through a lengthy process of releasing cash from his current investments, liquidating outstanding balances from the loans he had, and investing his capital with the firms he liked. He knew the whole thing would take time, but he was in no rush to be done. He was enthusiastic about the transition to a less-intensive workload. He was now well into his forties, had several interests, family, friends, etc., but above all, he now had two children whom he would enjoy having more time to spend with.

Almost two years went by before Oliver could finish the whole transition, but he was greatly relieved when he did. He kept a small part of his property portfolio because he was emotionally attached to some properties, and the time required to take care of them was almost nothing. He sold everything else for a profit, allowing him to be out of debt and with significant capital, which he invested in the two companies he selected.

Also, instead of investing with the third company he had originally liked, he decided to build a small portfolio of *REITS*, or real estate investment trusts. He liked that REITS were public companies that traded in the stock market, so buying and selling them was relatively quick and easy, but they also provided dividends. Oliver kept harvesting on his expertise by selecting several REITS he could foresee would be good investments. He analyzed the strategies they used, and the management teams employed.

Additionally, Oliver was able to gain access to areas he would not have been able to if he had continued investing the way he had before. Oliver invested in REITS that specialized in hotels, healthcare facilities, large-scale multifamily developments, and shopping centers. He now had less stress, more time, and amazing income.

He was very happy working as a board member with the local company he invested in. He basically acted as a consultant, but he didn't have to do all the tedious work that followed after strategic decisions. His interest in wine led him to buy a property in wine country, close to a beautiful little town, just a few hours' drive from their home. The family used the place as a vacation home, and Oliver developed the land as vineyards. He built a small wine manufacturing facility and enjoyed making his own wines. He put together a great team of local experts to develop his wines and started selling them pretty successfully, so again his vacation property became an investment with cash flow.

Oliver was content with the standard of living he had achieved. Natalie had developed a very successful online business, which allowed her to work form anywhere, and with both kids now in college, they enjoyed going back and forth between the city and their wine country homes. They also joined the country club in wine country, where Oliver enjoyed playing tennis and Natalie was learning to play golf. The whole family traveled together a couple times a year, skiing in the winter and seeking adventure in a new destination every summer.

Even though Oliver and his family had been on a continuous stretch of adding options and luxuries to their life, Oliver was very careful about the way he used his money. He had made a very detailed plan about how much he needed to continue investing every month based on his average historical returns. He wanted to make sure he could continue providing at least the same level of life his family had been able to enjoy. He had also sketched out how much he needed his income to be before he would allow himself to add any perk such as when they joined the country club, buying a new car, or what kind of vacation they would take that year.

Oliver also thought that he was happy being a real estate investor, as well as a stocks investor, but he decided he would only continue investing in companies that were socially responsible. He knew that idea would limit his investment options significantly, but he also was certain companies with such focus were managed by highly conscious people who typically were great businesspeople as well. In fact, Oliver realized such companies were not only good for the planet, but they also provided great returns.

Within the local real estate company he invested in and was a board member of, Oliver became an activist promoting eco-friendly developments. He kept insisting they install green technologies that would make the developments self-sufficient. Others were hesitant because they thought all those gimmicks would only bring the construction costs up, therefore driving the returns on investments down.

After a while, people on the board started agreeing with Oliver. The company started either building or enhancing their communities by providing rainwater tanks, solar panels, designated spaces for composting, and areas to grow food such as vegetable gardens and fruit trees, among other ideas Oliver kept promoting. Because of this trend, their developments became highly sought-after communities. They were able to charge a premium on rents, which made the returns on investments even better.

Oliver had proven his point, which strengthened his worth to the company's board, while also reinforcing his personal values and beliefs around his investments. He was not only concerned with the returns he was making but also with being of service to the community and in his way, helping make a better world. More than twenty years after he became an investor, Oliver had more concerns when it came to his investments outside of just making more money. He'd actually become more and more concerned with things such as social justice and ecological impact and less and less with investment values and returns.

Case Analysis of Stage 3: Sophisticated Skills, Sound Identity

Here is the analysis on this part of Oliver's story in relation to the sophisticated skills, sound identity stage of an investor's development.

Developmental Tasks

1. **Work discipline and management of life's demands.** In the third case study, Oliver has a young and growing family that requires attention, and he has many other things he likes doing. Of course, as he expands on his investments, work demands are only increasing as well. Oliver went

through a period of thinking about how to best organize all his time-constraining pursuits, especially after they were causing tensions with his wife. In his case, having work discipline meant finding a way to continue growing his investments without setting himself up for seventy-hour workweeks. It took a while, but he managed to shape things in a way where he gained a lot of free time again, was able to spend more time with his family, and even gained access to investments he had not previously considered possible.

2. **Lifestyle and investment plans.** As Oliver expanded his investments and his income grew, the family's lifestyle evolved. The sophisticated skills, sound identity stage lasted many years—Oliver kept renewing his investing plans, but he was always very disciplined about having attainable goals and sensical rewards; he never lost the edge on how he would continue building on his investment portfolios. Following through on investment plans is a task that is easier to achieve for someone with Oliver's background and personality. That does not mean this is true for everyone. Oliver was very clear he didn't want to have the issues his father had and made sure he didn't go anywhere near them. He also had ambition and likings that had high costs. Oliver knew and enjoyed that kind of life, but he also knew how to be responsible about having the benefits of an affluent lifestyle. He was very disciplined and concerned about never overreaching his capacities.

3. **Investment philosophy.** Oliver's investment philosophy evolved, as would be expected, throughout the sophisticated skills, sound identity stage. However, toward the end of the stage, he demonstrated clearly how and what he wanted out of his investments. At the beginning of the stage, Oliver was already highly identified with being a real estate investor and he continued with that, but how he engaged in such investments changed from a highly

demanding and time-consuming activity to a much more passive occupation. Oliver also went from being highly concerned with income to being more interested in having time to be with his family and to do the things he enjoyed. So he transitioned from being incredibly busy to prioritizing his relationships and interests. At the end of the stage, Oliver finally became a strong advocate of social responsibility. He wanted his portfolio to be focused on more conscious companies, and he kept endorsing that policy focus for the developments managed by the local company he was a board member of.

Investment Crisis: Expanding vs. Aridness

Oliver became a wildly successful investor. He was a very determined and highly ambitious individual with great abilities and capacities. It comes as no surprise that he resolved the stages crisis positively with a strong output of expanding. Nevertheless, he did go through a crisis that fostered his achievement of the tasks and his capacity to continue expanding.

Oliver was moving strongly in the direction of adding more residential units, but it was when he had tensions with Natalie and started thinking of alternative ways to manage his investments that he went into crisis. He really felt that if he didn't continue growing the way he was, he would not be able to increase his income right at a time where he could foresee high expenses on the horizon. That in turn meant for him the falling to pieces of what he had built and life as he knew it then. That feeling Oliver experienced was the force of aridness showing up to create the crisis that spun off the dynamic and boosted Oliver to do some heavy thinking and take action to transform things.

Oliver's resilience shined when he put together a new plan that not only allowed for him to continue growing his wealth but also enabled him to spend more time with his family and on other things he was missing. Oliver was able to transition to a more passive way of investing in his area of interest because of the level of expertise and network of contacts he had developed. Successfully being able to resolve the crisis, Oliver was now in a very comfortable living situation.

Central Process: Inventiveness

Oliver was able to resolve the stage's crisis in a positive way through inventiveness. His creativity was called upon several times during the stage of sophisticated skills, sound identity. And luckily, his ideas worked out very well. By calling on his own inventiveness, Oliver was developing one of the most valuable tools an investor can have.

The stage's crisis started when Oliver was somewhat over-whelmed with work, which was causing friction in his relationship with Natalie. Oliver deliberately started thinking about how he could make things better for him, and without having any kind of guidance, predetermined path, or anyone who could tell him how to resolve the situation, he came up with several solutions. His ideas worked out well, and the stressors were practically wiped out.

First, Oliver got an idea from someone about investing in private funds. After some thinking and research, he decided it could be a good alternative for him. He then did more research and due diligence, which brought him to create an integral plan of how he would like to proceed. He realized there were no formulas, and any plan an investor creates is unique and only works for the person who comes up with it.

Oliver also showed inventiveness when he became a board member of the local company. While he had never heard of anyone investing in a private fund and asking to become an active participant, he thought it would be an ideal solution for him. He discussed it and presented himself as a valuable addition to the company's team. They liked the idea, and the plan meant Oliver had hit a home run. He'd also become very proactive about green developments, so he kept insisting the company get into them. They were highly resistant at first, but once they gave in, these new developments proved to be successful.

Investor Adaptive Quality: Commitment

Oliver moved on from the sophisticated skills, sound identity stage having acquired the investor adaptive quality of commitment. He demonstrated how persistent he could be with his ideas and how not even difficult situations were going to slow him down. However, the adaptive quality came from consistently demonstrating dedication to his investments, continually drafting new plans to adapt to changing situations, constantly being concerned with the impact of his investments in his family and community, and strongly following his values and integrating them into his investing plans.

Oliver conceived an investment philosophy that came out of his beliefs and applied it to how he made his investments. Not only did he show consistency and integrity by following through with his philosophy, but he also became more rooted in his ideas as his investment journey progressed. His identity as an investor sharpened every day, which empowered him to be highly proactive in pursuing his vision.

CHAPTER 6
Stage 4: Weathered Investor

Developmental Tasks:
1. Embracing one's life
2. Adopting new roles and new investment perspectives
3. Getting future generations involved
4. Planning a legacy

Investment Crisis: Appeasement vs. Despondency

Central Process: Contemplation

Investor Adaptive Quality: Insight

Core Issue: Condescension

Every stage provides an opportunity for growth no matter the biological age nor the degree of advancement and expertise as an investor. Charlie Munger, who at the time of this writing is ninety-seven years old, is Berkshire Hathaway's vice president and has been Warren Buffet's partner for more than a half century. He recently said, "Those who keep learning will keep rising in life."

Psychosocial theory presupposes that every stage in life brings about new opportunities. However, the main theme at the weathered-investor stage is a search for personal meaning. By this stage, investors draw on all the skills they have built, all the competencies they have achieved, and the creativity they have enhanced to effectively problem-solve. The wealth of life and investing experience, the perspective on time, and the ability to adapt to crises will guide an investor's search to resolve questions about life's meaning as well as their interests in investing.

As conditions change over time, the motivations for investing evolve as well. Motivations that once might have been highly important such as increasing personal income or wealth, acquiring power and achievements, will likely give way to new intentions. Those new motivations could be a desire for deeper understanding, experimentation with new roles, or new perspectives looking into the future.

The tasks at the stage of weathered investor are slightly different from every other stage. The main difference lies in that, while this stage's tasks are about personal growth as all the others are, the growth in this stage does not come from perfecting investing strategies or increasing the knowledge base. Growth instead comes from the introspective process of reflecting on achievements, successes, triumphs, as well as disappointments and failures, only to clearly realize where one is situated and hopefully savor a deep sense of satisfaction.

Developmental Tasks

Embracing one's life

One of the challenges of coming into the advanced stages is accepting the reality of one's life. By now, there is enough evidence of what has been possible to accomplish, the successes and failures in the major tasks of the previous stages, and the capacity to actually reap benefits from the investments made this far. In addition, investors might have started their investing ride with overly fantastic expectations, which by now may have been deflated by facing reality and realizing what can actually be achieved.

At this point, the factor of time—the most important variable in any investment—is shorter when looking forward than in hindsight. That means that if things have not been evolving as planned, it would be incongruous to have expectations for things to change significantly now. Accepting the current and the past performance and realizations can be a very difficult challenge.

An investor will need to be able to take in certain areas of failure, crises they have lived through, and disappointments encountered in their investment journey. Investors need to incorporate these difficult experiences without becoming overwhelmed and developing a sense of inadequacy. This becomes especially hard when looking at these types of experiences in retrospect because the investor knows that some setbacks had a significant impact on their life and there is no way to change that.

Investors also must be proud of their achievements. No investor goes unscarred through a life of participating in endeavors that involve risk. However, if at least a majority of the developmental tasks have been achieved throughout their investment careers, investors will be able to rejoice in their successes more times than they will have to deal with adversities and failures. When they come into this advanced stage, in which a significant part is spent looking toward the past, they will be able to enjoy what they have been able to pull off.

In reality, the majority of investors who make it to this advanced stage generally have a high level of satisfaction, which usually goes for both their investments and their lives. Nevertheless, weathered investors with years of experience and solid investing skills continue to strive for new levels of success.

Investors' goals and needs might change over the course of this advanced stage, depending on their life situations. But instead of viewing life satisfaction in terms of facing the end of the game, weathered investors continue to create new personal and investment goals and reassess their satisfaction by means of how they are doing with their newly established goals.

Adopting new roles and new investment perspectives

Every stage of development brings changes to the role of the investor, but perhaps the major role changes come at this advanced stage. Chronological age is not directly related to the degree of maturity an investor has achieved, but for most people this advanced stage of investing expertise will come in later adulthood. At this point investors are typically undergoing significant life changes such as becoming grandparents, experiencing significant physiological changes, moving into retirement, perhaps becoming community leaders or senior advisers, and even facing the death of friends or encountering widowhood.

Investors who become grandparents undergo psychological changes derived from significant transformation in the family. Becoming a grandparent will bring the individual to reflect on their past, going all the way back to thinking about their own childhood as well as their parenthood. That trip though memory lane will bring forth personal and interpersonal themes that will very likely have an impact on their investing goals and perspectives. Some people become more engaged grandparents than others, depending on their cultures and family situations. The key point, though, is that becoming a grandparent significantly contributes to an individual's sense of purpose and worth.

Another aspect that can have an impact on a change of perspective is related to the investor's life partner. One of the most important components in a successful investing journey is having a supportive life partner. That does not mean a person needs to be married to be a successful investor, but statistically a majority of adults do get married. According to Statista, 61.96% of adults in 2019 in the US stated they are married. Also, 15% of couples are unmarried but cohabitating.[31] That makes an overwhelming

---

[31] "Number of Married Couples in the United States from 1960 to 2019," *Statista*; Benjamin Gurrentz, "Living with an Unmarried Couple Now Common for Young Adults." United States Census Bureau.

majority of people who have an intimate partner who hopefully is supporting their journey.

Having to face the loss of a devoted partner can have a psychological impact on an investor's outlook for their endeavors. Plans can significantly shift by not having someone to share the benefits of a lifetime of building a portfolio of what are by now profitable ventures (hopefully).

One more factor that can have an impact on the view of the investments is retirement. Choosing to stop working means not receiving income from active work anymore, which means it will be time to fully live from the investments made so far. If things went as planned, the investor should have enough money from their investments to be able to sustain the lifestyle they have built. But fully depending on the investments to live adds pressure to the performance of such investments.

Adopting new roles and new perspectives will be challenging. Forming perspectives on the investments, their course, their results, and when and how the benefits can and will be enjoyed is a continuous process that starts as soon as an individual becomes an investor. In this late stage, it will be time to actually harvest what has been growing for a while, and to do that, a new perspective must emerge. The underlying essence of the new perspective is that it is not time to grow anymore but time to garner what was planted.

Getting future generations involved

Following along the reasoning that the majority of people have families, investors fall into the category of having families as well. Investors have come to a point where they will begin to think about the future in a particular way, one that involves their families perhaps even more than their concern for themselves. By this stage, the family has typically grown to a point of having several generations. With multiple generations in the family, one of the perspectives investors start to consider is bringing their relatives into what has been their longtime, personal development.

This task does not apply to every investor in the same way, but it does apply to everyone. Some investors decide never to get married or have a family, and there might not be generations to follow. Nevertheless, people in such a case will need to get others involved in the management of their investments and wealth created for their heritage to continue after their passing (more on that topic will follow in the next task). For people in this case, the personal growth of achieving the task of getting future generations involved comes from setting up the correct team that will effectively carry on with the investor's wishes when they can no longer be the one executing their own plans.

Research coming out of the field of family business suggests that getting the next generation involved and successfully educating them for a transition cannot be successful unless the person who has been leading (in this case the investor) realizes this is an inevitable event.[32] At the same time, the resistance to accepting this reality is a normal and natural reaction from the system—the system meaning both the investor and the family.[33]

Yet getting future generations involved in an investment process is generally easier than bringing them into an operating business. There are many reasons for this, but one of the most significant is that investments can be gradually moved into a more and more consolidated and passive situation. That allows for the investor to not only keep track of his investment decisions in perpetuity but also to be involved in the decision-making process if they decide to do so.

---

[32] Alexandra Solomon et al., "'Don't Lock Me Out': Life-Story Interviews of Family Business Owners Facing Succession," *Family Process*.

[33] Barbara Dunn, "The Family Factor: The Impact of Family Relationship Dynamics on Business-Owning Families during Transitions," *Family Business*.

The same cannot be said for an operating business where involving family dynamics into the business becomes incredibly complex. Intergenerational conflicts may arise. There is always resistance to change from the business. And the transition from one manager to the next can be such a significant event that sadly the majority of family businesses collapse at this intersection.

It is important that a clear distinction be made if what has been built is a business or a portfolio of investments. Over time it is easy to get confused, but if there is an infrastructure of an operational team of professionals managing the investments, then it is more likely that what has been developed is a business. That means that involving the next generations needs to be well thought out and executed. Otherwise there is the risk of becoming statistic by being a part of the great majority of family businesses that don't survive the intergenerational transition. If there is a portfolio of passive investments, however, then involving the next generation means educating the family about the investor's trajectory, decisions, results, philosophy, and ongoing affairs.

Planning a legacy

At this stage, the investor has to begin considering the inevitable fact that they won't live forever. Thinking about finitude of life brings about an instinctual reaction of a wish for immortality that usually gets acted on by educating their heirs, actively fostering a family culture with an intent of continuity, and the distribution or planning of inheriting the material goods and wealth created.

There are many aspects to consider and plan for when deciding about what to do with the material wealth that has been created, but a legacy goes by far beyond the financial achievements of the investor. The most important aspect of this task is reflecting on what the investor wants their legacy to be. A legacy is not only based on material goods. In fact, that's usually the least important aspect for the person thinking about what they want to happen to their possessions after their passing.

What is really important is the process of thinking deeply about how a person wants to be remembered after they are gone. The teachings that can be made and the examples that can be set are important. Passing on knowledge and experience and certainly fostering the right values and life philosophy in others is what truly builds a legacy.

Of course, one important aspect to plan for is what should happen to the wealth created by the investor's ventures. This is the time to not only decide but also make the necessary legal processes that will ensure the investor's desires will be followed. The most common case is that the investor decides to leave whatever they have accumulated to their family, but it should be in writing. Perhaps there is no family, and the investor wants their wealth to go into supporting a cause or different causes they believe in, which should be organized as well.

Finally, there are legal and tax implications of intergenerational transfer that should be planned for as well. Developing the most tax-efficient strategy ensures the majority of what the investor has created goes toward their designated receivers. Legal documents to support the whole plan should also be in place. This is important to provide peace of mind to the investor. That way the investor knows they have gone through the process of thinking, deciding, and executing what is required so they can be at peace with someday not being there. Even when planning for the end, the peace that can be brought to the investor by going through this final process can provide personal growth once more.

Investment Crisis: Appeasement vs. Despondency

In this advanced stage of weathered investor, the investment crisis derives from being at peace with what the investor has been able to achieve, as opposed to a downhearted, disappointed self for not having met expectations. The investor's expectations might have been unrealistic since the beginning, but the real issue usually is that the investor has had trouble accepting themself, their abilities, and their available resources. Therefore, they keep building on a fantasy that usually only leads to disappointment, glum, and depression.

This is a time of thinking back often, but memories may be altered to fit the current reality or current events may be reinterpreted to fit memories. *Appeasement* is the ultimate psychological accomplishment, as it provides a sense of meaning in life, and it gives purpose for the long and exhaustive work that the investor has put in.

To achieve appeasement means that the investor has developed the ability to accept the facts of what they have been able to build and can reconcile their investing trajectory with the hopes and dreams they may have had years before. Obtaining appeasement comes from integrating all the investment crises that have come earlier, as well as all the investor adaptive qualities and core issues that have accumulated through the investing journey.

Appeasement really is very closely related to finding the meaning of the investor's life, but it can only come after significant introspection. Most people have some regrets. It's easy to look back and think about a missed opportunity, a bad decision, or a poorly managed situation. The challenge is to view the past experiences with acceptance. It's through that process that people usually find meaning to their stories and make sense of their life.

On the opposite side of the spectrum there is *despondency*, or hopelessness. Not to be pessimistic, but it's quite often that people resolve the crisis of appeasement versus despondency in the negative direction. To resolve the crisis in the positive direction, investors need to integrate a lifetime of failures, issues, and disappointments as well as the successes and achievements to create a data-informed plan. They must face what is referred to as the "death of dreams," a realization that some of their most highly valued hopes for themselves and their families cannot be accomplished in their lifetime.[34]

Weathered investors who did not accomplish what they expected or even what is recognized by their social group as acceptable may face some degree of devaluation and even hostility from their community. The negative attitudes these investors can encounter in family members, colleagues, or younger investors can be perceived as the investor's lack of competence, or their general failure. That can certainly make anyone feel discouraged about their self-worth. Despondent investors are at risk of falling into major depression mostly because they know there is no way to compensate for past failures at this point.

Central Process: Contemplation

To *contemplate* means to look thoughtfully at something. In order to resolve the weathered investor's crisis, the weathered investor needs to engage in an introspective, self-contemplative process that requires significant effort, and it must be done individually. Sometimes it may even require temporary isolation to enable the investor to reminisce on the long-term memories of the investment journey the individual has had.

John Meacham, a professor of psychology at the State University of New York whose work has focused on memory, described the process of reminiscence as having four elements:
- The selection of an event to review
- Immersion in the details of the story, including the strong emotions linked to the event
- Withdrawal from the past by distancing oneself from the event or comparing past and present

---

[34] Wayne E. Oates, "Reconciling with Unfulfilled Dreams at the End of Life," in *The Aging Family: New Visions in Theory, Practice, and Reality.*

- Bringing closure to the event by unearthing a lesson or making an observation.[35]

This process helps a person build a bridge between the past and the present and is linked to positive adjustment in advanced stages.

People who are able to go through this process are generally better adapted to their reality and have better outlooks of life. However, not all reminiscence is positive. Obsessing on the past and past mistakes is not productive and will not bring the same benefits of well-being that a naturally contemplative process will. Usually when there is obsessive reminiscence, it's because there's too much guilt about past events that is still lingering, and the investor has not been able to accept, integrate, make meaning, and/or let go of such events.

Overall, contemplation has a positive value and is a process that can help integrate past and present experiences. It supports meaning making and provides growth to an investor in an advance stage. Without the proper contemplative process, the investor will not be able to achieve these valuable insights.

Investor Adaptive Quality: Insight

A positively resolved conflict through the process of contemplation will provide the investor with the adaptive quality of insight. When an investor has developed *insight*, they have the power of seeing into a situation, and they intuitively understand the inner nature of familiar things because they have focused on developing an expertise. They also usually have a sophisticated level of self-awareness, which further supports their abilities to see and understand things clearly.

---

[35] John A. Meacham, "Reminiscing as a Process of Social Construction," in *The Art and Science of Reminiscing: Theory, Research, Methods, and Applications.*

An insightful investor has a heightened capacity to deal with difficult situations and resolve hard questions; they can also quickly adapt to complex situations. Usually they can do this because they have accumulated significant knowledge on the facts involving their area of expertise. They also know the procedures they need to follow to resolve complex situations; they have a broader base to contextualize the issues they are facing.

Having insight is also related to having clarity about one's values and goals. When such lucidness is attained, it's easy to recognize if an opportunity is well aligned with one's values and goals or not. If it's not, then it is easy to let go of it with no conflicting feelings or thoughts. And when the opportunity is aligned with the investor's values and/or goals, then at this point, the investor will rely on the knowledge and experience to seize the prospect.

Finally, an insightful investor has developed the ability to recognize and manage uncertainty. All investors need to take a bit of a leap of faith when delving into a new investment. There is always a certain degree of uncertainty to what the future will hold for such project, but the wiser and more experienced the investor is, the easier it is for them to understand and manage the unknown that lies ahead.

Core Issue: Condescension

Those investors who fail to achieve enough insight are at risk of becoming condescending. *Condescension* derives from a narcissistic personality that stems out of probably being financially secure but not having really achieved all the tasks of personal development. Psychologically, a *narcissistic personality* in an individual is an inflated sense of the importance of themselves. They have a deep need for attention and admiration and always lack empathy for others. But what really lies behind this mask is a fragile self-esteem that feels helpless against external criticism.

Now at the end of the road, condescending investors need to show their grandiosity because deep down they feel a significant internal void, and they know there is no way they can change their pasts. They unconsciously have the need to react vigorously to this sentiment that makes them feel inferior by acting with a pompous attitude and trying to fill the void with material goods and arrogant attitudes.

An insightful investor is flexible in their thoughts, and they are open to new ideas and interpretations because they understand the complexity of life. In contrast, an investor who falls into condescension constantly rejects other ideas and repudiates most people. They usually behave projecting an air of superiority that denotes their inner sense that their ideas and opinions are better than anyone else's.

All these traits typically create problems in many areas of life, starting with relationships, but also in work and business. In the case of an investor, developing such attitude can shut doors and have an impact on the investor's professional network and investment opportunities. But most importantly, not going through a successful introspective process of contemplation means they will not be able to accept themself and the outcomes of their investing trajectories, which in turn will make them sad and bitter.

No one wants to find themself in the final stretch feeling unaccomplished. Fortunately, insight can be achieved by engaging in the central process of contemplation, which when resolved positively will provide the investor with insight.

CASE STUDY 4

Further Up the Ladder

By his mid-sixties, Oliver had done well for himself. He had a nice family with children who were already adults and well on their way to building their own careers. He had a couple of great homes—one even operated as a wine business, and he enjoyed spending time there. He had a great relationship with his wife, who was also a successful entrepreneur. Financially, he had excelled with his investments and was happy participating on the board of the local real estate company where he had become one of the main investors. The company had also become the top-producing real estate investment firm in the area.

Both of Oliver's parents had recently passed away. Oliver had never been able to rekindle his relationship with his father, but he had helped out for years by paying for his father's retirement community. His father had developed severe dementia and was not well because of his years and years of alcoholism. Oliver's mother had kept closer to him and his family, and she had even continued investing alongside her son and was happy with the income he was creating for her. She was an active woman who even in her late eighties had kept up her work and activities, but unfortunately she had a massive heart attack and passed away suddenly.

Oliver's older daughter, Charlotte, had pursued a career in the food industry, where she trained as a chef and had had the opportunity of working under some great master chefs in several countries. She had developed a passion for agriculture as well and decided to go back home and ask her father for support to open a restaurant in wine country near their home. Charlotte wanted to grow her own fruits and vegetables for her kitchen and buy the rest of the supplies from local farmers. Of course she would also strongly promote her father's wines in the restaurant.

Oliver and Natalie were ecstatic that after so many years away, their daughter had decided to come back and settle down where they lived. They were also a little perplexed, as she had been living and working in the south of France for several years. Once she came back, she told them she had gone through a bad breakup with her French boyfriend and she preferred to be back home, where she could see herself long term.

When Charlotte presented the whole plan for her restaurant, Oliver did not even flinch. As soon as she was done, he said he would certainly invest with her. He'd also learned a thing or two about local farmers and the food industry in wine country by producing and selling his wines. He knew he'd be able to help his daughter get started in more ways than just being a sponsor with money.

After reviewing the business plan, Oliver agreed that the first thing Charlotte needed to do was to start looking for a lot. She needed to be able to grow her supplies as well as build her restaurant. Oliver was no stranger to searching for real estate, but this time he wanted to allow Charlotte to do the footwork. He could easily have taken over that part of the project but was wise enough to not undermine Charlotte; it was her plan to lead. It was only when Charlotte asked that Oliver referred her to the local Realtor he'd worked with when he bought his wine country estate.

When Charlotte called the agent, she said she had retired recently but that her son Scott had taken over her business and could help with her search for a lot. Charlotte talked to Scott, and he seemed to understand exactly what she needed. He had a few suggestions for her, and after a while of going back and forth with emails of maps and pictures of land, he said they should go on a tour to see a few options. Charlotte was very excited and became even more so when an attractive young guy showed up to take her see the lots. They spent the whole day driving around wine country and had a very pleasant day. They also saw a couple of interesting locations for Charlotte's restaurant.

Since Charlotte was living with her parents for the time being, Scott dropped her off home at the end of the day. Oliver noticed what was going on when he saw Charlotte getting of the car. Oliver asked Charlotte how her search went and she said, "Wonderful!"

He asked, "Did you see anything you like?"

She said, "Yes."

"Well, which lot did you like?"

"I can't remember!"

Oliver just laughed and said, "Okay, I understand." And understand he could, perhaps more than she knew, but he didn't say a word.

Charlotte was very determined and sharp, just like her father. In the next several days she kept reviewing the information on the couple of locations she did like and went to visit them with her parents. She decided on a location, and Oliver agreed it would be the best option, so they bought the land. In the meantime, Scott had been going above and beyond in helping Charlotte purchase the lot. One day, Oliver told Charlotte, "You know, I've had my share of dealings with Realtors. I've never seen one so dedicated."

After the closing, Charlotte and Scott started dating. Charlotte also started working on the restaurant. It took a couple of years for Charlotte to develop the restaurant and the land, but she had been able to start harvesting some of the things she had been planting and was finally ready to open the restaurant. She and Scott had been dating all that time and had decided to move in together. Charlotte had a little house built in the same lot where the restaurant and her crops were, so they planned on living there.

When the restaurant opened, it did not bring in enough people at first. Apparently Charlotte's menu design was a bit too out there for the local market. But Charlotte kept going, invested in marketing, and after about a year, the restaurant started to have a following. They finally went out of the red and became profitable. Charlotte resorted to different strategies she had learned in the restaurants she had worked at before. And after the second year, her restaurant became a destination for foodies. Around that time, Charlotte and Scott decided to get married.

All the while, in a distant science institute, Oliver's younger son, Leo, had become an academic and full-time researcher. He had two PhDs and no intention of ever leaving the academic life. Oliver's relationship with him had always been a little more complicated— they were not too close but not too distant either. Perhaps they were less compatible due to their distinct personalities.

Leo was also incredibly ambitious like his sister. Within the academic environment where he felt comfortable, Leo had achieved an amazing reputation, becoming one of the youngest tenured professors at the institute. He had a PhD in molecular biology and a PhD in cellular biophysics, and he was doing research on fundamental cell processes and looking at developing computational models of cellular metabolic control and molecular switches. Oliver was incredibly proud of Leo and had been happy to sponsor his Ivy League education all the way through his second PhD. But he just didn't understand Leo very well.

A couple years after Charlotte and Scott's wedding, the whole family went on a trip. As they were having dinner one night, Charlotte announced she and Scott were having a baby. Oliver and Natalie cried tears of joy, and the whole trip became a celebration. Oliver was also stunned—he couldn't believe he was going to be a grandfather. He suddenly felt the whole world change before his eyes.

When he started thinking about finances, he realized his investments were not just for covering his family's expenses or supporting them in their endeavors anymore. Amazingly, he felt his responsibilities had just multiplied. He trusted his daughter to be a successful entrepreneur and responsible parent and thought his son-in-law was okay too. But he still had a feeling that he needed to be ready for anything, and now that included three generations. For a while, that feeling triggered Oliver to constantly review his whole financial situation and to think often about his trajectory as an investor.

The grandbaby was born, and everything went well with Charlotte and the baby. Charlotte had a baby boy who would grow up among the orchards, vines, and the restaurant kitchen. Charlotte was lucky enough to live just a few steps from her restaurant, which made it easy to care for her baby and keep an eye on things at the restaurant. Oliver and Natalie were lucky to be grandparents who lived just a stone's throw away, which turned out to be highly convenient.

Everything was going great when one morning Charlotte rushed out of the house searching for Scott. Concerned by her panic, he asked what was wrong.

She gave him the baby and said, "I'm going to the hospital. It's my father—he had a heart attack."

By the time Charlotte got to the hospital, Oliver had been stabilized. He had to stay in the hospital for a few days, but he was out of danger. Leo flew in and stayed for a few days. The doctors did not have a good explanation about the root cause of the problem; they said Oliver was a healthy guy with good habits, so they could only attribute the heart attack to genetics.

Oliver was quite shaken by the event. He spent some time at home recovering and thinking he needed to have some things in line in case something as such happened again and he was unable to recover. He spent significant time reminiscing about his endeavors, achievements, current standing, and what he wanted for his family. He needed to write a will, but it wasn't the legal aspect that had him concerned. He was instead concerned that his children know about his investments.

Charlotte and Leo had a vague idea of what Oliver had in terms of his investments. They certainly knew about what he did through all the stories they grew up listening to. They knew how he became an investor, all the difficulties he ran into, the times when he was desperate and how their mother helped him, how he got back on the saddle again, and how he became a respected member of the real estate investment community.

Oliver recovered and went back to his usual lifestyle, but he had a different perspective. It was when Charlotte had her second child that Oliver decided to ask Charlotte and Leo to sit down with him to talk about his assets. They organized a family meeting in the wine country house. Leo took a week off to have time to spend with his family and attend his father's summoning.

While the meeting was a bit stressful, especially for Charlotte and Leo, it also turned out to be a great opportunity for all of them to connect and learn about each other. Oliver had prepared a presentation describing each and every investment and asset he owned. Leo was particularly bewildered when Oliver started talking about his stock portfolio, his current positions, and of course all the history surrounding the construction of that portfolio. Oliver was amazed that Leo understood every single thing he was describing, even the technical language.

In the meeting, Oliver was very thorough when describing his real estate portfolio. He explained everything to everyone, current positions, income, expenses, who they should contact for whatever reason, etc. As Oliver had centered his investment lifespan around being a real estate investor, this was the central topic for the meeting. He then spent the rest of the week telling stories about how he built his portfolio, mishaps, tenant issues, and other adventures he had gone through with all his properties. It was an outstanding meeting and a very pleasant week.

Oliver later discovered that Leo followed along well because Leo had been building a portfolio of his own. Academics did not have such a high income, but Leo had helped out a couple of biotechnology startups. He had been paid in company shares, and one of them became incredibly successful, rendering an astonishing return on Leo's shares. Leo sold his shares and had been building a stock portfolio. In fact, he had developed a proprietary algorithm that signaled when he should buy and sell stocks. He had been yielding amazing returns on his investments.

This was the first time Oliver had heard of all this, but he was in such high spirits that this event completely turned around his relationship with Leo. They started talking a lot more often, and Leo kept sending Oliver his algorithm's recommendations so Oliver could try out the system. Oliver was very pleased with what the algorithm could do and especially with his son's developments and interests.

After the meeting, Charlotte also agreed to get involved with the wine business. It made sense for her to become an active participant when she was already in the agriculture and food business. She actually knew a lot about wines and in particular her father's wines, as she lived nearby the vineyard, which was also her parents' home. Charlotte had spent significant time there, knew everybody, and knew the wines well because she always had them at her restaurant.

Charlotte got more involved in the management of the whole operation. However, for her, this was business and not just a hobby as it had been for her father. She continued to expand the business by buying more land to harvest different grape varieties and to buy grapes from other local producers. She also developed new labels and increased production, marketing, and distribution. Charlotte even started participating in international wine competitions and earned several awards, which brought their labels to be better-known, making them easier to sell at higher prices.

As time went by, Oliver was very pleased to see how both of his children started becoming more and more involved with his investments. He decided to make family meetings a regular thing. In fact, he had been reading some literature on family business and decided to formalize things a little more. While he was an investor and they did not operate a family business, he considered that investments should be taken as seriously as any other job. He also attributed a significant part of his success to having followed that philosophy throughout his investment journey.

When Oliver turned eighty, he was aware of his decaying strength and energy. He was very satisfied with what he had built and was glad he had asked his children to become more active with him. They now had a formal family counsel that had regular monthly meetings. They had a family constitution outlying their values, principles, general vision, and goals as well as how they made decisions and new investment policies. The document considered every branch of the family, including grandchildren, who, by the way, were getting close to going to college.

Oliver was overall content with what he had been able to do with his life. He knew he was at a point where he could see far behind his timeline but didn't have too much more to expect when looking forward. He was glad things were working out and continuing to grow. And he was pleased not much depended solely on him anymore. He'd become very active with a couple of foundations where he volunteered to help with their missions, and of course, he was also an important donor. Natalie and Oliver moved permanently to their home in wine country, where they foresaw spending whatever time they had left.

Case Analysis of Stage 4: Weathered Investor

Here is the analysis of the conclusion of Oliver's story in relation to the fourth stage of an investor's development, further up the ladder.

Developmental Tasks
1. **Embracing one's life.** In this stage there are a few times in which Oliver realizes his situation has changed, which

throws him off a bit, but also prompts him to take new perspectives. There are instances when he looked back with a sense of satisfaction, such as having supported his father regardless of his father's situation or their relationship. He kept close with his mother and brother and helped them get started with investing as well. Oliver always provided for his family as best as he could. He thought about the difficulties he'd run into, but he was glad he had support from loved ones to move on. Also, he more than made up for his financial loses in his lifetime, so thinking about that helped him feel better about his bad calls. He set up new goals for this stage, such as educating his family and working for foundations. He came to realize his time in this world, as well as his energy, were winding down. With the time he had left, Oliver wanted to keep doing what he knew best.

2. **Adopting new roles and new investment perspectives.** This stage brought about a mature Oliver who was concerned with providing for his family. He was interested in helping his daughter set up a business and in supporting long years of costly education for his son. Of course, the big paradigm shift came when he became a grandfather. As he thought about having a grandchild, Oliver got a sudden sense of added responsibility along with a renewed sense of purpose. He was instinctively, unconsciously, and primitively feeling he was not just a father anymore—he was becoming the leader of a tribe. Given his acute sense of responsibility, Oliver felt this was a time to be prepared and felt a need to be present, aware, and ready for whatever came their way.

3. **Getting future generations involved.** This task was a major thing in Oliver's case. After his scare with the heart attack, he decided to get his children involved with his investments. Bringing the children in proved to be an incredibly

enriching experience for everybody. Oliver and Leo's relationship evolved and improved to be better than ever, and Charlotte flourished as an entrepreneur by strongly enhancing the wine business. Things went so well that they even formalized the family gatherings and family participation in the investments. That action allowed the family to function very well as a team and even have the grandchildren considered for future involvement.

4. **Planning a legacy.** When Oliver asked his children to sit with him to learn about his investments, he was clear and outspoken about them knowing what he had and where. At the time, it was mostly as a precaution in case anything should happen to him. What he did not explicitly say was that he was also planning for continuance. He got both Charlotte and Leo involved with the real estate investments, which had been Oliver's main development throughout his investment journey. He got Charlotte involved with his wines and Leo with his stock portfolio. When they structured the family council, one goal was to oversee how the wealth was going to keep moving down the generations. Oliver was deliberately planning how his assets should be managed moving forward. He was truly delighted to see the day came when he was appreciated but not needed. He had successfully gotten the next generation involved and organized his legacy to the point he was just there to enjoy the remainder of his time with them.

Investment Crisis: Appeasement vs. Despondency

This stage's crisis is brought upon through looking back into what the investor's trajectory has been. The investor knows there is no going back with past decisions, and there is not much time to look forward to either. In Oliver's case, he felt the stress of the stage's crisis when he learned he was going to be a grandfather. He trusted his daughter and son-in-law to become competent and responsible parents, but Oliver still had a feeling that he needed to be ready to face whatever came their way.

Embracing the feelings of his responsibility came through Oliver questioning his capability to provide for his family, which by the stage of weathered investor was growing into a third generation. Oliver's self-inquiry raised his level of awareness to where his was and about what he had built throughout his investment endeavors.

Oliver had two main goals for his investments from a young age. He wanted to be able to live comfortably from his investments without having to keep a day job, and he wanted to not fall into his father's footsteps. He wanted to be able to sustain the lifestyle he was able to provide to his family, which hopefully could keep improving over time. Oliver was aware that he'd been able to achieve both goals, but he'd never considered a third generation in the family. He went into the stage's crisis when he realized his situation but was able to resolve it relatively soon and in a positive way because he had in fact achieved his goals and been quite prolific with his investments.

Oliver felt furthermore appeased when after reviewing and reviewing his finances, he prepared his presentation for his family and invited them to get involved. It was then that he was able to explicitly see and transmit how fortunate he was, how successful he had been overall, and what a privileged financial situation he found himself in. He became more conscious that he had achieved a wonderful skillset, an excellent ability to make decisions, a particular position among his peers, but above all, an emotional maturity that had allowed him to build the amazing assets portfolio he had.

Central Process: Contemplation

Oliver goes through the central process of contemplation a few times in the stage of weathered investor. Every time Oliver became contemplative, it was because some event pushed him into reassessing his trajectory and situation. A scary episode like his heart attack had a strong effect on Oliver's perspective on his life, and the joyful event of having a grandchild shook him a bit as well.

Oliver took the time to evaluate his life, his personal journey, family situation, financial positions, and personal developments. After he went through the heart episode, he actually dedicated some time to think and reminisce by himself about his life. He also reflected on what he wanted from the time he had left to live. He came out of the introspective process with a clear intention of integrating his family with what so far had been his world—the world of investments.

Investor Adaptive Quality: Insight

Having positively resolved the stage's crisis, Oliver acquired the investor adaptive quality of insight. The main driver to become an insightful investor is undergoing the process of contemplation. Oliver was propelled into a contemplative state a few times in the stage, but he embraced each instance and came out the other end with heightened insight.

While this stage's description does not delve that much into the technicalities of Oliver's dealings and new investments, it is clear that he became an amazingly capable investor who developed a deep understanding of his areas of expertise. It's also easy to perceive that through the appreciation he developed in the company where he was a board member. The fact that he was able to steer the whole company into investing through what had become his investing philosophy denotes the respect experts in the real estate investment industry had for him.

Obviously, such degree of recognition can only be reached by someone who has demonstrated a certain level of abilities. However, technical skills were not enough for someone to be recognized and followed as Oliver was. Oliver became an insightful investor, as seen from his strong capacity to adapt to difficult situations, his increasing ability to put perspective on things, and the intuition to identify the best strategy to follow into a successful resolution.

References

Adler, Alfred. "The Fundamental Views of Individual Psychology." *International Journal of Individual Psychology* 1, no. 1 (1935): 5–8.

Brickman, Philip, Dan Coates, and Ronnie Janoff-Bulman. "Lottery Winners and Accident Victims: Is Happiness Relative?" *Journal of Personality and Social Psychology* 36, no. 8 (1978): 917–927.

Campbell, James. "What an Economist Means by Rationality." Economics on Hippo Reads, 2015. http://read.hipporeads.com/what-an-economist-means-by-rationality/

Cassidy, Jude. "The Nature of a Child's Ties." In *Handbook of Attachment: Theory, Research and Clinical Applications*, edited by J. Cassidy and P.R. Shaver. New York: Guilford Press, 1999.

Conlin, Michael, Ted O'Donoghue, and Timothy J. Vogelsang. "Projection Bias in Catalog Orders." *American Economic Review* 97, no. 4 (2007): 1217–1249.

Dunn, Barbara. "The Family Factor: The Impact of Family Relationship Dynamics on Business-Owning Families during Transitions." *Family Business Review* 12, no. 1 (1999): 41–57.

Einstein, Albert. (March 24, 1954). Albert Einstein to J. Dispentiere, AEA 59–495.

Elert, Glenn. "What is Work?" *The Physics Hypertextbook*, 2021. https://physics.info/work/.

Englis, Basil G., and Michael R. Solomon. "Where Perception Meets Reality: The Social Construction of Lifestyles." *Values, Lifestyles, and Psychographics* (1997): 25–44.

Epstein, Seymour. "Cognitive-Experiential Self-Theory." In *Advanced Personality*, edited by David F. Barone, Michel Hersen, and Vincent B. Van Hasselt, 211–238. Boston, MA: Springer, 1998.

Epstein, Seymour. "Cognitive-Experiential Self-Theory: An Integrative Theory of Personality." In *The Self with Others: Convergences in Psychoanalytic, Social, and Personality Psychology*, edited by Rebecca Curtis, 111–137. New York: Guilford Press, 1991.

Epstein, Seymour. "The Self-Concept Revisited: Or a Theory of a Theory." *American Psychologist* 28, no. 5 (1973): 404–416.

Erikson, Erik H. *Adulthood.* New York: W. W. Norton and Company, 1978.

Erikson, Erik. H. *Childhood and Society.* New York: W. W. Norton and Company, 1963.

Erikson, Erik H. *The Life Cycle Completed: A Review.* New York: Norton, 1982.

Freud, Sigmund. "Three Essays on the Theory of Sexuality." In *The Standard Edition of the Complete Psychological Works of Sigmund Freud, Volume VII (1901-1905): A Case of Hysteria, Three Essays on Sexuality and Other Works*, 123–246.

Freud, Sigmund. (1930). "Civilization and its Discontents." In *The Standard Edition of the Complete Psychological Works of Sigmund Freud, Volume XXI (1927-1931): The Future of an Illusion, Civilization and its Discontents, and Other Works*, 57-146.

Friedman, Debra, and Barry R. Weingast. "Rational Choice and Freudian Accounts of Cooperation." https://ssrn.com/abstract=2390255.

Greenfield, Patricia M., Heidi Keller, Andrew Fuligni, and Ashley Maynard. "Cultural Pathways through Universal Development." *Annual Review of Psychology* 54, no. 1 (2003): 461–490.

Gurrentz, Benjamin. (2018, November 15). "Living with an Unmarried Couple Now Common for Young Adults." United States Census Bureau. https://www.census.gov/library/stories/2018/11/cohabitaiton-is-up-marriage-is-down-for-young-adults.html.

Havighurst, Robert J. *Developmental Tasks and Education.* Chicago, IL: University of Chicago Press, 1948.

Havighurst, Robert J. *Human Development and Education.* New York: Longmans, Green, 1952.

"Investor." *Cambridge Advanced Learner's Dictionary & Thesaurus,* Cambridge, UK: Cambridge University Press, 2021. https://dictionary.cambridge.org/dictionary/english/investor.

Kahneman, Daniel. *Thinking, Fast and Slow.* New York: Macmillan, 2013.

Kermer, Deborah A., Erin Driver-Linn, Timothy D. Wilson, and Daniel T. Gilbert. "Loss Aversion Is an Affective Forecasting Error." *Psychological Science* 17, no. 8 (2006): 649–653.

Laslocky, Meghan. "How to Stop Attachment Insecurity from Ruining Your Love Life." *Greater Good Magazine,* February 13, 2014. https://greatergood.berkeley.edu/article/item/how_to_stop_attachment_insecurity_from_ruining_your_love_life.

Loewenstein, George, and Daniel Adler. "A Bias in the Prediction of Tastes." *The Economic Journal* 105, no. 431 (1995): 929–937.

Meacham, John A. "Reminiscing as a Process of Social Construction." In *The Art and Science of Reminiscing: Theory, Research, Methods, and Applications,* edited by Barbara K. Haight and Jeffrey D. Webster, 37–48. Philadelphia: Taylor & Francis, 1995.

Milad, Mohammed R., and Gregory J. Quirk. "Neurons in Medial Prefrontal Cortex Signal Memory for Fear Extinction." *Nature* 420, no. 6911 (2002): 70–74.

Moore, Christopher. *Socrates and Self-Knowledge*. Cambridge, UK: Cambridge University Press, 2015.

Morgan, Maria A., and Joseph E. LeDoux. "Differential Contribution of Dorsal and Ventral Medial Prefrontal Cortex to the Acquisition and Extinction of Conditioned Fear in Rats." *Behavioral Neuroscience* 109, no. 4 (1995): 681–688.

Morgan, Maria A., Lizabeth M. Romanski, and Joseph E. LeDoux. "Extinction of Emotional Learning: Contribution of Medial Prefrontal Cortex." *Neuroscience Letters* 163, no. 1 (1993): 109–113.

Murphy, Barbara, and Glen W. Bates. "Adult Attachment Style and Vulnerability to Depression." *Personality and Individual Differences* 22, no. 6 (1997): 835–844.

Newman, Barbara M., and Philip R. Newman. *Development through Life: A Psychosocial Approach*. 10th ed. Belmont, CA: Wadsworth Publishing, 2009.

"Number of Married Couples in the United States from 1960 to 2019." *Statista*. https://www.statista.com/statistics/183663/number-of-married-couples-in-the-us/.

Oates, Wayne E. "Reconciling with Unfulfilled Dreams at the End of Life." In *The Aging Family: New Visions in Theory, Practice, And Reality*, edited by Terry D. Hargrave and Suzanne M. Hanna, 259–269. New York: Brunner/Mazel, 1997.

Quirk, Gregory J., Gregory K. Russo, Jill L. Barron, and Kelimer Lebron. "The Role of Ventromedial Prefrontal Cortex in the Recovery of Extinguished Fear." *Journal of Neuroscience* 20, no. 16 (2000): 6225–6231.

Quirk, Gregory J., René Garcia, and Francisco González-Lima. "Prefrontal Mechanisms in Extinction of Conditioned Fear." *Biological Psychiatry* 60, no. 4 (2006): 337–343.

Rick, Scott, and & Lowenstein, George. "The Role of Emotion in Economic Behavior." In *Handbook of Emotions*, edited by Lisa F. Barrett, Michael Lewis, and Jeanette M. Haviland-Jones, 138–156. New York: The Guilford Press, 2010.

Shiller, Robert J. "How About a Stimulus for Financial Advice?" *New York Times*, January 17, 2009.

Shiller, Robert J. *Irrational Exuberance*. Princeton, NJ: Princeton University Press, 2000.

Shorey, Hal. "Come Here, Go Away: The Dynamics of Fearful Attachment." *Psychology Today*, May 26, 2015. https://www.psychologytoday.com/us/blog/the-freedom-change/201505/come-here-go-away-the-dynamics-fearful-attachment.

Snyder, Charles R., Jennifer Cheavens, and Susie C. Sympson. "Hope: An Individual Motive for Social Commerce." *Group Dynamics: Theory, Research, and Practice* 1, no. 2 (1997): 107.

Snyder, Charles R. "Hope Theory: Rainbows in the Mind." *Psychological Inquiry* 13, no. 4 (2002): 249–275.

Solomon, Alexandra, Douglas Breunlin, Katherine Panattoni, Mara Gustafson, David Ransburg, Carol Ryan, Thomas Hammerman, and Jean Terrien. "'Don't Lock Me Out': Life Story Interviews of Family Business Owners Facing Succession." *Family Process* 50, no. 2 (2011): 149–166.

Vygotsky, Lev. *Mind in Society: The Development of Higher Psychological Processes*. Cambridge, MA: Harvard University Press, 1978.

ABOUT THE AUTHOR

Born and raised in Mexico City, Dr. Fainsilber was an entrepreneur leading several highly successful businesses before becoming an investor. In his entrepreneurial journey, he encountered significant setbacks. But the difficult times served to strengthen his abilities and enabled him to become a prosperous investor. He has now built over 20 years of investing experience. Additionally, Dr. Fainsilber has spent over a decade working with individuals and families who are searching for ways to enhance their lives emotionally and financially.

Dr. Fainsilber has a strong academic background with degrees in industrial engineering, business, counseling psychology, and clinical psychology, as well as other certifications. His education spans many of the best academic institutions across the world. He currently resides in the little town of Valle de Bravo, Mexico, with his family.

Can You Help?

Thank you for reading my book!

I really appreciate all of your feedback,
and I love hearing what you have to say.

I need your input to make the next version
of this book and my future books better.

Please leave me an honest review on Amazon
letting me know what you thought of the book.

Thanks so much!

Dr. Ricardo Fainsilber